WOOTTON

THE GIANT AIRSHIPS

TIME
LIFE ®
BOOKS

THE GIANT AIRSHIPS

by Douglas Botting

AND THE EDITORS OF TIME-LIFE BOOKS

TIME-LIFE BOOKS, ALEXANDRIA, VIRGINIA

Time-Life Books Inc.
is a wholly owned subsidiary of

TIME INCORPORATED

FOUNDER: Henry R. Luce 1898-1967

Editor-in-Chief: Henry Anatole Grunwald
President: J. Richard Munro
Chairman of the Board: Ralph P. Davidson
Executive Vice President: Clifford J. Grum
Editorial Director: Ralph Graves
Vice Chairman: Arthur Temple

TIME-LIFE BOOKS INC.

MANAGING EDITOR: Jerry Korn
Executive Editor: David Maness
Assistant Managing Editors: Dale M. Brown (planning),
George Constable, Martin Mann, John Paul Porter
Art Director: Tom Suzuki
Chief of Research: David L. Harrison
Director of Photography: Robert G. Mason
Assistant Art Director: Arnold C. Holeywell
Assistant Chief of Research: Carolyn L. Sackett
Assistant Director of Photography: Dolores A. Littles

CHAIRMAN: Joan D. Manley
President: John D. McSweeney
Executive Vice Presidents: Carl G. Jaeger,
John Steven Maxwell, David J. Walsh
Vice Presidents: George Artandi (comptroller);
Stephen L. Bair (legal counsel); Peter G. Barnes;
Nicholas Benton (public relations); John L. Canova;
Beatrice T. Dobie (personnel); Carol Flaumenhaft
(consumer affairs); James L. Mercer (Europe/South Pacific);
Herbert Sorkin (production); Paul R. Stewart (marketing)

THE EPIC OF FLIGHT

Editorial Staff for *The Giant Airships*
Editor: Thomas H. Flaherty Jr.
Designer: Donald S. Komai
Chief Researcher: Pat S. Good
Picture Editor: Jane N. Coughran
Text Editors: Russell B. Adams Jr., Lee Hassig
Staff Writers: Malachy Duffy, Thomas A. Lewis,
C. Tyler Mathisen
Researchers: Susan Schneider Blair (principal),
Betty Ajemian, Patti H. Cass, Cathy Gregory, Sara Mark,
Carol Forsyth Mickey, Dominick A. Pisano
Assistant Designer: Van W. Carney
Editorial Assistant: Kathy Wicks
Art Assistant: Anne K. DuVivier

Editorial Production
Production Editor: Douglas B. Graham
Operations Manager: Gennaro C. Esposito, Gordon E. Buck
(assistant)
Assistant Production Editor: Feliciano Madrid
Quality Control: Robert L. Young (director), James J. Cox
(assistant), Daniel J. McSweeney, Michael G. Wight
(associates)
Art Coordinator: Anne B. Landry
Copy Staff: Susan B. Galloway (chief), Elizabeth Graham,
Cynthia Kleinfeld, Victoria Lee, Celia Beattie
Picture Department: Rebecca C. Christoffersen
Traffic: Jeanne Potter

Correspondents: Elisabeth Kraemer (Bonn); Margot
Hapgood, Dorothy Bacon, Lesley Coleman (London); Susan
Jonas, Lucy T. Voulgaris (New York); Maria Vincenza Aloisi,
Josephine du Brusle (Paris); Ann Natanson (Rome). Valuable
assistance was provided by Nakanori Tashiro, Asia Editor,
Tokyo. The editors also wish to thank Helga Kohl, Martha
Mader (Bonn); Brigid Grauman (Brussels); Karin B. Pearce
(London); Carolyn T. Chubet, Miriam Hsia, Christina
Lieberman (New York); Dag Christensen (Oslo); M. T.
Hirschkoff (Paris); Mimi Murphy (Rome).

THE AUTHOR

English writer Douglas Botting's romance with lighter-than-air flight began with a balloon safari across Africa. Since then he has focused on the airship, producing several film histories for the British Broadcasting Corporation and participating in an abortive airship expedition over Greenland. He has met many of the luminaries of the airship era whose stories appear in this book. *The Giant Airships* is his sixth Time-Life book.

THE CONSULTANT for The Giant Airships

Douglas Robinson saw his first dirigible at the age of five when the U.S.S. *Shenandoah* flew over his home in Weston, Massachusetts. He became a practicing psychiatrist, but his early fascination with airships nurtured a lifetime of research that has earned him international standing as an airship authority. His writings include *The Zeppelin in Combat, Giants in the Sky* and *LZ 129 "Hindenburg."*

THE CONSULTANTS for The Epic of Flight

Melvin B. Zisfein, the principal consultant, is Deputy Director of the National Air and Space Museum, Washington. He received degrees in aeronautical engineering from the Massachusetts Institute of Technology and has contributed to many scientific, technological and historical publications. He is an Associate Fellow of the American Institute of Aeronautics and Astronautics.

Charles Harvard Gibbs-Smith, Research Fellow at the Science Museum, London, and a Keeper-Emeritus of the Victoria and Albert Museum, London, has written or edited some 20 books and numerous articles on aeronautical history. In 1978 he served as the first Lindbergh Professor of Aerospace History at the National Air and Space Museum, Smithsonian Institution, Washington.

Dr. Hidemasa Kimura, honorary professor at Nippon University, Tokyo, is the author of numerous books on the history of aviation and is a widely known authority on aeronautical engineering and aircraft design. One plane that he designed established a world distance record in 1938.

For information about any Time-Life book, please write:
Reader Information
Time-Life Books
541 North Fairbanks Court
Chicago, Illinois 60611

Library of Congress Cataloguing in Publication Data

Botting, Douglas.
  The giant airships.
  (The Epic of flight; 6)
  Bibliography: p.
  Includes index.
  1. Air-ships—History. I. Time-Life Books.
II. Title. III. Series: Epic of flight; 6.
TL657.B67   629.133'24'09   80-12128
ISBN 0-8094-3272-2
ISBN 0-8094-3271-4 (lib. bdg.)
ISBN 0-8094-3270-6

CONTENTS

Vessels to navigate the oceans of the air

The air, said Sir George Cayley in 1816, is "an uninterrupted navigable ocean that comes to the threshold of everyman's door." The eminent aeronautical pioneer was depicting a tantalizing vision of future flight; the "ocean," however, needed a practical ship of the air to ply it, and as Cayley's century ended, none existed. The airplane had not yet been invented, and balloons—more than 100 years after their introduction—still could not get to anyone's door unless the wind was exactly right.

A few determined men held that the best hope for controlled flight was a motorized, steerable balloon: the dirigible. A number of these had been tested, but each was underpowered or unreliable or both. Then, as the 20th Century began, the accelerated development of lighter metals, more suitable fabrics and the internal-combustion engine gave impetus to the dream of a lighter-than-air ship that could be navigated anywhere. The quest for the right combination of design, power and material enlivened the skies over several nations.

The challenge was to build a dirigible that was streamlined enough to move easily through the air, large enough to lift a practical payload of men and machinery, yet sturdy enough not to buckle in mid-flight. The French in 1902 solved the problem in part by adding a rigid keel to an elongated envelope (opposite) and distributing the weight of the payload over its entire length. Theirs was the first of a series of semirigid airships of increasing size, speed and endurance that—sometimes at least—could be counted on to reach a specified destination.

These early craft had a distressing tendency to rip, to run into things, to be carried away by high winds and, on tragic occasion, to catch fire. Yet optimism in their future persisted—nowhere more than in the stout heart of a German nobleman, Count Ferdinand von Zeppelin. Zeppelin was past middle age when he made the creative leap that revolutionized dirigibles: away from the balloonlike envelope shaped primarily by the pressure of the gas that filled it, to a permanent, rigid hull of vast size, and thus vast lifting power.

With Count von Zeppelin's experiments began the age of the giant air ship, and an adventure that was unique in the history of flight. His mammoths of the sky would bring the miracle of long-distance air travel—and the destructive missiles of war—virtually "to the threshold of everyman's door."

Workmen dismantling the Paris Exposition in 1903 watch as line handlers move the airship Lebaudy I. Nicknamed Le Jaune for the protective yellow coat of lead chromate on its cloth envelope, it introduced the rigid keel to airship design and is considered the first practical dirigible.

An artist's rendition shows the British Army's first dirigible, the Nulli Secundus, or "Second to None," cruising London in 1907. Wide silk straps around the envelope supported a tubular steel framework on which were mounted the open car and the control and stabilizing surfaces.

A Parseval short-range reconnaissance airship flies over the German countryside in 1909. The nonrigid dirigibles performed so well that by 1914 Parsevals had been purchased by the armies of seven nations.

Arriving over London from Paris on the 16th of October, 1910, the French-built Clément-Bayard II becomes the first airship to make the flight from the Continent. The dirigible had covered 244 miles in six hours.

Stopped by engine failure, head winds and fog in an attempt to cross the Atlantic in 1910, the crew of the airship America lowers its lifeboat near a rescue vessel, the steamship Trent. The America had flown for 71½ hours, a new endurance record.

1

The Count's unshakable dream

All through the first weekend of July 1900, festive crowds of Germans, Austrians and Swiss had waited patiently at the town of Manzell on the German shore of Lake Constance to see the maiden flight of Count Ferdinand von Zeppelin's long-vaunted airship. Small dirigibles had flown before, but the Count's was the first with pretensions of practicality—a monstrous machine, it was said, as high as a church and as long as an oceangoing steamer. At least 6,000 people had assembled at lakeside and another 6,000 had taken to the water in a flotilla of private motor launches, chartered yachts and commercial passenger steamers to have a closer look at the great floating hangar in which the airship was housed. All waited expectantly for the historic moment: peasants in *Lederhosen,* heavily whiskered burghers, stiff Prussian generals and ministers from Berlin, a Bavarian princess and—perhaps most important—a commission of officers from the Prussian Army Airship Battalion, charged with reporting on Count von Zeppelin's invention to Kaiser Wilhelm himself.

Inside the hangar every part of the airship had been checked and checked again. The 17 huge gas cells suspended inside the aluminum framework of the airship's rigid, cigar-shaped hull had been inflated with hydrogen. Almost 800 pounds of water ballast had been pumped on board and distributed fore and aft so that the ship floated level just above the long pontoon raft to which it was tied. Rudder lines had been inspected and the two Daimler engines—each driving a pair of small propellers—had been tested. Nothing had been overlooked.

For two days a blue flag was raised to half-staff atop the floating hangar, signaling that the winds were too high to risk a flight. Twice the crowd went home disappointed. But those who came a third day were rewarded; by late afternoon on Monday, July 2, the surface of the lake had smoothed and the wind had diminished to a whisper. At 6:30 p.m. the word was passed: "Airship ready for takeoff." Count von Zeppelin, a stout 62-year-old ex-cavalry commander with a white walrus mustache, twinkling eyes and a white yachting cap perched on his round head, asked for silence before leading the assembled airshipmen—and the local gymnasts, firemen and soldiers who had volunteered as handlers—in prayer. Then he and his four crewmen boarded the two boat-shaped aluminum gondolas slung below the towering hull.

Count von Zeppelin and his companions were setting off into the unknown. No airplane had yet flown. The Count's rigid, multicelled

Count Ferdinand von Zeppelin, portrayed at left in a German magazine in 1908, had been a brigadier of cavalry before he turned full time—and with unwavering determination—to developing his concept for the rigid dirigibles that eventually became synonymous with his name.

behemoth was totally unlike any successful airship that had preceded it, and Count von Zeppelin—who many thought was a prime candidate for a lunatic asylum—was almost as untried as his ship. His knowledge of flying came from a few ascents he and his crew had made in balloons to accustom themselves to the sensations of being airborne. Their knowledge of powered flight was entirely theoretical. But to Count von Zeppelin the risks were not out of proportion to his goal: "I am not a circus rider who performs for the public," he had told a reporter. "I am doing serious work for my country."

At 7:30 p.m. a steam tug took the airship's raft in tow and carefully extracted the dirigible from the hangar onto the open lake. Count von Zeppelin had chosen to operate from the water because of the broad open space it offered and because he thought the impact of a hard landing would be less there than on land. Moreover, the airship hangar, anchored only at the closed end, would always swing away from the slightest breeze; this prevented the airship from being blown against the side of the hangar as it emerged under tow.

The ground crew was directed by the senior member of the Kaiser's inspection commission, Captain Hans Bartsch von Sigsfeld of the Airship Battalion, which normally operated the German Army's tethered observation balloons. Hand over hand they payed out the handling lines; the airship, bathed in a golden sunset, rose 100 feet above the raft. From the forward gondola the Count shouted: "Let go the lines." A new chapter in the history of flight had begun.

Almost immediately, as the airship rose from the lake, it was clear that something had gone awry. The line handlers at the bow of the airship had responded promptly to the Count's order to let go, but the men at the stern had not heard it clearly and had held onto the lines a few seconds longer. Consequently, as the airship drifted away on a newly risen breeze, its nose pointed sharply skyward. Electing not to trim his ship until it was under power, the Count ordered the engines started. The one in the rear gondola, operated by mechanic Albert Gross and a journalist named Eugen Wolf, fired first, followed by the one in the forward gondola, which was shared by the Count, his physicist friend Baron Konrad von Bassus and an engineer named Friedrich Burr. As the airship's propellers bit the air and the craft gained headway, Wolf, the official reporter for the flight, had time to note: "Majestically, free of every shackle, the airship floats away and the thousandfold hurrahs of the crowd echo from the shore as slowly she makes way to the south."

From the lake, the huge airship was a fabulous sight—a colossus of the skies that seemed to symbolize the soaring ambitions of the German nation at the beginning of a new century. The spectators fell silent as the great shape gradually drew away from them under the steady threshing of its four propellers; the ship made a turn to starboard, then to port, and climbed to a height of some 1,300 feet. "Everyone must have formed the impression that it was not the blind chance of the elements that sent it on its way," wrote Wolf, "but the highest expression of human will."

On board the airship, however, all was not as it should be. Once the engines were started, the Count's first concern had been to level the airship by lowering its bow, a maneuver he accomplished by vigorously winding forward a 220-pound lead weight slung on a cable beneath the ship. But when he tried to crank the weight to its neutral position amidships, it jammed. With the weight now locked in a forward position, the bow of the ship dropped below the horizon and the engines began to propel the dirigible toward the lake. The Count released water ballast forward to lighten the nose, but still the aircraft descended. Only by ordering the propellers into reverse was he able to keep his vessel airborne. To complicate matters, one of the engines failed.

Zeppelin had no alternative but to land. At 8:21 p.m., with considerable skill, he settled the huge craft gently onto Lake Constance near the steamer landing at the village of Immenstadt, three and a half miles from where it had taken off. The first flight of the first Zeppelin airship had ended only 18 minutes after it had begun. "What this short flight will lead to is not completely clear," wrote the journalist Wolf. "But one thing it did show—dirigible flight is a reality."

The Kaiser's commission was less than enthusiastic. The airship, they reported, was "suitable for neither military nor nonmilitary purposes." On the evidence of the flight they had witnessed—short, erratic and slow (its top speed had been only eight miles per hour)—the Kaiser's observers could hardly have reported otherwise.

But the white-haired Count, with reserves of resourcefulness and persistence unknown in most men half his age, refused to give up. He rebounded from this semifailure—and from others that followed—and before he was finished he had dragged himself, his stately aircraft and an incredulous world into the age of the great airships.

The era lasted from that first halting flight in the summer of 1900 to the dismantling of the last Zeppelin in 1940, and saw the Count's grand monsters and others like them set one aeronautical precedent after another. Airships became the first commercial aircraft, conveying paying passengers across the German countryside for years before airplanes carried anyone but a pilot and crew. They delivered the first major wartime aerial bombardment, dropping their explosives on London, Paris and several other European cities in World War I. An airship crossed the Atlantic Ocean a few weeks after the first airplane and was the first aircraft of any kind to cross from east to west, against the prevailing winds. Airships carried explorers across the frigid wastes of the Arctic, and in 1929, in luxurious fashion, one of them circumnavigated the world in 21 days; the first globe-girdling airplanes, a few years earlier, had required eight times as long.

By the late 1920s airships were regents of the skies, far surpassing even the radically improved airplane in capacity and comfort, and outpacing steamships in speed. In those years, the airplane and the airship seemed destined to complement, rather than preclude, each other. Airplanes had proved superior for fast flights over short distances, while the greater range and payload of airships made them the ultimate in air travel over longer distances.

Yet airships, with their vast surfaces, were vulnerable to high winds and bad weather. More than one of the dirigibles fell victim to turbulences that airplanes would have survived. Such accidents provided fuel for the airships' detractors, who argued that there was something inherently and irremediably wrong with them. The majestic giants continued to fly and to prosper, although it will never be known how long they might have endured in the face of ever-higher construction costs and the rapid improvement in airplanes effected by World War II. As Count von Zeppelin's creation seemed to be approaching its full potential, it was suddenly transformed—during 32 seconds of horror over an airfield in Lakehurst, New Jersey, in 1937—from a machine that dreams are made of into a real-life nightmare.

"The vehicles," wrote Dr. Samuel Johnson from his deathbed in 1784, "can serve no use till we can guide them. I had rather now find a medicine that can ease an asthma." The renowned man of English letters referred of course to free balloons, in which only a year earlier men had inaugurated the era of flight. No thoughtful person could contradict him. If only balloons could be made dirigible, that is, steered under their own power, the world would be revolutionized. Journalists and cartoonists, indulging in flights of fancy, foresaw balloon taxis plying the airspace above city streets, intercity balloon stagecoaches and a worldwide network of balloon passenger transports. Some of these visions were far from impracticable, but it would take more than a century before they were achieved.

From the outset, large numbers of scientists and showmen, engineers and aristocrats, eccentrics, charlatans and fools devoted themselves to the challenge of making a balloon dirigible. Clearly such a craft needed power to propel it and a rudder to steer it by. If ships of the sea had sails, should not ships of the air have them too? And oars, or paddles, as well? Why not wings that flapped like a bird's, or perhaps real birds to pull the balloon through the sky like an aerial coach-and-four? Why not cube-shaped balloons that would collapse into a single-plane surface and glide along the air currents like a kite?

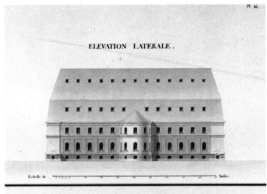

ELEVATION LATERALE.

Without exception, such analogies to ship, bird and kite proved unworkable, and aeronauts soon turned to the inventions of the industrial age. They attempted to drive a balloon with paddle wheels, using manpower and airborne horses. They proposed the reactive forces of steam jets, compressed air, gunpowder and primitive rocketry. They even designed a screw-shaped airship that was meant to bore through the air as a bit cuts through wood. None of these ideas helped divert the balloon from its wayward and helpless course before the wind.

The failures of science in no way deterred some imaginative charlatans from making outlandish claims of success. In 1834 a company called the European Aeronautical Society opened the world's first air-

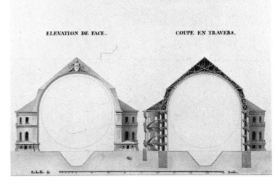

ELEVATION DE FACE.   COUPE EN TRAVERS.

These 1785 watercolors by French soldier-engineer Jean-Baptiste-Marie Meusnier detail his revolutionary—and still-valid—concept of an ellipsoidal dirigible (above), streamlined to reduce air resistance, and a peak-roofed hangar (left) to house it.

line office in Golden Square, Soho, London, to sell tickets for a regular passenger airship service between London and Paris. The aircraft was to be an oar-powered dirigible named the *Eagle,* built by a French colonel of Scottish descent who called himself the Comte de Lennox. Unfortunately, the *Eagle's* first prototype burst during inflation in Paris and was torn to pieces by an angry mob, some of whom had invested in the project. The second was seized in London by the sheriff and carted off in wagons when the airline company, not surprisingly, went bankrupt.

From time to time, however, among all the fallacious concepts, one inventor or another would make a significant and lasting contribution to airship design. As early as 1783, the year of the first man-carrying flights, a brilliant French Army engineer, Jean-Baptiste-Marie Meusnier, realized that to be steerable a balloon would have to be made streamlined; he designed an elongated envelope with a number of features that later were applied to practical airships. One of these was the ballonet, a bladder placed inside the envelope of a balloon. Pumped full of air, a ballonet expanded and contracted to maintain pressure in the envelope and keep it from buckling.

In 1816 two Swiss living in England, John Pauly and Durs Egg, designed (but never finished building) a dolphin-shaped dirigible with a weight attached that could be moved fore and aft to trim the craft for level flight, lower the tail to ascend, and depress the nose to descend. Laughed at as "Egg's Folly," it nevertheless was the first application of a principle that would become standard practice in later dirigibles. The next year Sir George Cayley, the inventive Englishman who is recognized as the father of modern aeronautics, proposed the airscrew, or propeller, as the best means of pushing a dirigible through the air.

By the middle of the 19th Century, most basics of airship design—streamlined envelope, rudder, ballonet, propellers, trim weight, even a load-bearing keel—had been worked out. What was lacking was an engine strong enough to push the craft forward against the wind, yet light enough to be lifted into the air by balloon. In 1852 Henri Giffard of France took the first step toward that goal.

Two years earlier, Giffard, a leading designer of steam engines, had witnessed the flight of a clockwork-powered model dirigible, built by a French clockmaker, that bore a prophetic resemblance to the great rigid airships of the following century. The model captivated Giffard, who determined to fly in a dirigible airship of his own design, driven not by clockwork but by steam.

On a September day in 1852 Giffard, dressed for the occasion in a top hat and frock coat, climbed into a gondola suspended below a keel-like pole that in turn was suspended from a balloon 144 feet long. At the rear of the pole a triangular sail was used as a rudder. Giffard shared the gondola with 500 pounds of coke and a steam boiler and 3-horsepower engine of his own design that together weighed another 350 pounds. In front of a large and astonished crowd he chugged away from the Paris Hippodrome at a steady six miles per hour—slower than the speed of a contemporary stagecoach—and disappeared from view over the suburbs of Paris. For 17 miles Giffard puffed through the air, undeterred by the slight but ever-present risk that a spark from the boiler might ignite the 88,000 cubic feet of inflammable gas in the envelope above his head. His safe landing at Trappe marked the success of the first powered flight in history.

Giffard's solo flight was a milestone, but it scarcely heralded the conquest of the air. He had demonstrated that he could steer downwind with his rudder, and on a subsequent flight he turned his craft in a circle, but his steam engine was not powerful enough to fly against the wind. In 1883 the French aeronauts Gaston and Albert Tissandier twice flew an electrically powered airship, but it too was underpowered. The next year, Charles Renard and Arthur Krebs, both engineering officers in the French Army, developed a lightweight battery that made possible the first flight in which an aircraft returned to its takeoff point. Their 23-minute, five-mile circuit in *La France* proved that navigation through the air was possible—though just barely.

The factor that eventually made dirigible flight practical was the internal-combustion engine. When such an engine was first tried in a dirigible by a German engineer, Paul Hänlein, in 1872, it was found to be too heavy and feeble. But it was later improved on by his country-man Gottlieb Daimler. The first aerial experiments with Daimler's engine were performed by Karl Wölfert, a German clergyman-turned-professional balloonist. Wölfert made one brief flight in 1888, but nine years later his experiments ended tragically when the open flame required by Daimler's ignition system ignited the hydrogen in Wölfert's airship, turning it into a funeral pyre for him and his mechanic.

In Paris, during those same years, an unusual young man was developing a highly personal airship, with which he would enthrall the French public. Powered by a tiny engine with an electrical ignition system and fired by spark plugs, it was safer to operate near hydrogen.

Alberto Santos-Dumont was born in Brazil in July 1873, the son of a prosperous coffee grower. A child of slight physique, with a reserved, dreamy disposition, he was an odd boy whose curiosity about the machinery on his father's plantation was equaled by his fascination with the science-fiction fantasies of Jules Verne. Balloonists were his heroes, as was the engineer Henri Giffard, who had built the steam-powered airship. "In the long, sun-bathed Brazilian afternoons," Santos wrote later, "I would lie in the shade of the veranda and gaze into the fair sky of Brazil, where you have only to raise your eyes to fall in love with space and freedom. So, musing on the exploration of the aerial ocean, I too devised airships and flying machines in my imagination."

Such impractical reveries were considered distinctly eccentric in agrarian Brazil. But in Paris, which Alberto first visited with his father for seven months in 1891, the young man found himself in a more sympathetic atmosphere, for Paris at the end of the 19th Century was

The evolution of dirigible design

The three basic types of airship construction are shown below. The simplest design was nonrigid. It had no fixed internal structure; its shape was maintained by internal gas pressure, which in turn was regulated by varying the pressure in air-filled bags, called ballonets *(dashed lines),* inside the envelope. These single-celled nonrigids often buckled under the strains of heavy weather or heavy loads.

The problem was partially solved by adding a lightweight keel *(shown in blue)* along the bottom of the envelope to cre-

ate a semirigid ship. The keel took some of the stress off the envelope by distributing the weight load more evenly, permitting the construction of larger ships.

Count von Zeppelin took the next step, designing an envelope held rigid by a metal skeleton attached to a sturdier keel *(drawing at bottom).* As the envelope no longer needed internal pressure for its shape, the gas could be housed in a series of self-contained cells *(partial cutaway)* wired into place—a safer and more efficient arrangement.

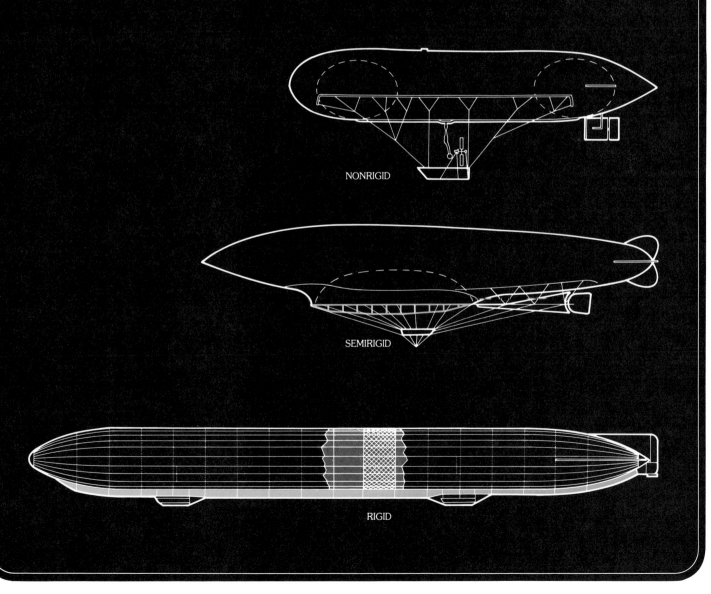

NONRIGID

SEMIRIGID

RIGID

the hub of Western civilization, a magnet for artists, writers, musicians, scientists and engineers.

In 1892 Santos' father, in failing health, bestowed a share of the family fortune on his son. Alberto returned to Paris and single-mindedly applied himself to the task to which he had secretly pledged his life—the conquest of the air. He engaged a tutor and embarked on a private course of self-education in the sciences necessary for such an undertaking. He lived alone, modestly but in the best part of town. He eschewed female companionship and the distractions of Paris' social whirl in favor of complete dedication to his goal.

Santos made his first ascent, in a hired balloon, in 1897. Taking off near Versailles one spring morning, he entered a new world that was to him as entrancing as his boyhood dreams. The stillness and smoothness of the balloon's rise, underscored by the unfamiliar view of the earth so far below, fascinated him beyond measure. Between bites of cheese and sips of champagne, he wrote, "I observed the pilot at his work, and comprehended perfectly all that he did. It seemed to me that I had been born for aeronautics." Santos, who stood a little more than five feet tall and weighed 110 pounds, promptly ordered a balloon built to his own specifications—a one-man craft of varnished Japanese silk with a gas capacity only one seventh that of a conventional balloon. In it, before attempting powered flight, he set out to learn such techniques of the balloonist's art as the balancing of gas and ballast to achieve equilibrium in the air, and the controlled accident known as landing.

By the end of 1897, Santos was an accomplished aeronaut with some 25 ascents behind him. During that winter he began work on the design of his first airship. A frankfurter-shaped balloon, it was fitted with a triangular silk rudder in front for steering, a weight-balance system for changing altitude and a basket far below the envelope to carry the inventor and his simple air-cooled engine, the creation of a French aristocrat-engineer, the Marquess Albert de Dion. Santos had used the engine first on a small three-wheeled motorcycle that had carried him through the streets of Paris at speeds up to 20 miles per hour. It exerted 3½ horsepower, weighed only 66 pounds and almost always ran when required to. It was fitted to a propeller with shovel-shaped blades.

The construction of Santos' Airship No. 1 proceeded through the summer of 1898. On September 18 he had it inflated with hydrogen for its first test flight. A small crowd of enthusiasts, including a number of experienced balloonists, gathered at the new Zoological Gardens in the Bois de Boulogne for what proved to be an instructive debacle. Dressed in a flying ensemble that consisted of a dark suit, a shirt with a high, stiff collar, a silk tie and a cloth cap, the diminutive Brazilian stepped into the tiny basket, where the engine was warming, and cried "Let go all!" He had wanted to take off into the wind, but the veteran balloonists present had talked him out of it. Take off downwind, they advised, as one would in a balloon. He did, and the wind, augmented by the churning propeller, carried Santos crashing into a cluster of trees before he could gain

Inventor and fashion plate (he made high collars popular in Paris), Alberto Santos-Dumont is portrayed in the gondola of his first airship. The paddle-bladed propeller was powered by an engine adapted from his three-wheeled motorcycle.

enough height to clear them. Lesson No. 1, he decided, was that all powered craft must take off into the wind.

Two days later, after repairing the minor damage sustained by his ship, he put this lesson into practice. Headed into a gentle breeze, Airship No. 1 lifted off; Santos hauled in the forward weight and the ship's nose pointed skyward, chugging gently over the trees. Then Santos pulled on the rudder line and the nose came around. With its rigging twanging and its basket creaking, the ship performed a circle above the considerable crowd gathered below. Santos was gripped by an ecstasy such as he had never known.

"My first impression," he wrote later, "was surprise to feel the airship going straight ahead. It was astonishing to feel the wind in my face." But it was the "utterly new sensation of movement in an extra dimension" that made the deepest impression on Santos. He wrote: "I cannot describe the delight, the wonder and intoxication of this free diagonal movement onward and upward, or onward and downward, combined at will with brusque changes of direction horizontally when the airship answers to a touch of the rudder."

The ecstasy, however, quickly turned to dismay. Looking up, he discovered that the gasbag was sagging in the center; a pump that he had counted on to replace lost gas with air was not up to the task. Santos shouted to some boys, who were flying kites in the park, to grasp the drag rope dangling from his car and run with it into the wind. "For the moment," he recalled later, "I was sure that I was in the presence of death." But the boys slowed his fall, and he survived this landing, as he was to survive many others. Though his airship was badly damaged, he was buoyed by a conviction that he was on the right track.

In his study in Rue Washington, Santos continued to calculate, plan and design. He built two small dirigibles, and by the end of 1899 his ships had become familiar sights over the rooftops of Paris. With every flight his reputation grew: His tremendous verve and courage, his exoticism and his charm drew crowds wherever he appeared. His name became a household word—"le petit Santos," the French affectionately called him. High society flattered him, and in Brazil, his home country, he was fast becoming a legend.

The 20th Century was four months old when Santos' aerial ambitions took on a new focus. In April 1900, at a meeting of the Aero Club in Paris, a wealthy financier, oil tycoon and sportsman named Henry Deutsch de la Meurthe announced that he would commemorate the new century by establishing a lucrative prize. He offered 100,000 francs to any airman who could fly from the Aero Club's headquarters at St. Cloud, just outside Paris, to the Eiffel Tower and back, a total of seven miles, in no more than half an hour.

This was a daunting challenge; in Germany, Count von Zeppelin was still preparing his mammoth airship for its first test, and in France there was only one man, Santos, who had any hope of making the flight. Santos reckoned that to cover the assigned course in 30 minutes would require a speed of 14 miles per hour in still air, and a good bit more than that if there was a wind. His Airship No. 3, with a top speed of 12 miles per hour, was too slow, so he set to work on a new one. Built for speed, Airship No. 4 had no basket; Santos steered it with handlebars while perched on a bicycle seat that, like the engine, was attached to a longitudinal pole slung beneath the envelope. But even this ship was too slow, so he enlarged the envelope for increased lift and switched to a new 15-horsepower engine.

The resulting Airship No. 5 boasted a sturdy, triangular-shaped keel, made of pine and 60 feet long. The keel was suspended from the balloon and had the pilot's basket attached to it near the bow, the engine near the center and the propeller at the stern. Santos made his first attempt to win the Deutsch Prize with Airship No. 5 in July 1901. He reached the Eiffel Tower, but on the return leg to St. Cloud the new engine stalled and he crashed into a chestnut tree on the Rothschild estate. Santos was found in the tree by a footman who climbed up a ladder with a picnic hamper to succor the stranded aviator.

A second attempt the following month fared even less well. Once more, Airship No. 5 reached the tower, but when it began to lose gas through a defective valve on the return leg, the ballonet he had installed inside the envelope failed to compensate for the loss. "The ship fluttered in the air and flopped alarmingly," wrote an eyewitness, the correspondent of London's *Daily Express*. "Santos-Dumont was being tossed on great wind swells in a wrecked airship! The stem sagged, and the propeller, still slowly revolving, caught in the supporting piano wires. There was a ripping and a rush of gas. With a sickening, despairing flop the airship began falling."

Santos tried to maneuver to a landing in the Seine, but at the last moment the envelope caught on a chimney pot atop the Trocadero Hotel and burst. The keel and basket dangled precariously by their wires several stories above the ground. Santos climbed onto a window ledge and was rescued by the local fire brigade amid the cheers of the crowd below. He was intact, but Airship No. 5 was a total loss.

At this moment of public failure, Santos displayed his extraordinary resilience. Working day and night, he and his crew of mechanics and workmen built a new ship, No. 6, in 22 days. Except for a more powerful engine, it was scarcely distinguishable from its predecessor. On October 19, 1901, after several false starts, Santos was ready for a fresh assault on the Deutsch Prize.

The weather was blustery during the night and Santos did not sleep well. In the morning, winds of 11 miles per hour at the Eiffel Tower tempted him to postpone the flight; on the return to St. Cloud, the wind would be in his face. Speed had become even more of a challenge because of a change in the contest rules imposed by chauvinistic French officials, in the hope that if they could hold Santos off this time one of their countrymen might be able to overtake the Brazilian and win the prize for France. The 30-minute time limit remained, but the flight

His airship dangling in shreds after ripping on a hotel rooftop during his second try for the Deutsch Prize, Santos perches on a window ledge as firemen lower a rope.

would now be timed from launch to landing, rather than from start to flying finish. If Santos did not win in October he probably would not have another opportunity until spring.

At 2:30 p.m. the Brazilian started the engine; 12 minutes later he gave the order "Let go all!" and the official timekeeper started his watch. With a helping wind, the ship climbed crabwise with its nose steadfastly pointed toward the Eiffel Tower, visible against a bank of dark clouds. "The machine flew across the Seine," wrote a reporter from the *London Daily News,* "keeping as straight as an arrow. As it came abreast of the Tower it seemed a little speck."

Airship No. 6 reached the tower and completed its turn only nine minutes after takeoff. The crowd below gave a great cheer, women waved their handkerchiefs and men raised their umbrellas in salute and tossed their hats into the air. With 21 minutes left in which to return to St. Cloud and land, it seemed certain that Santos would win the prize, even with the wind against him. But 500 yards from the tower his engine began to misfire and slow down. Santos was seen climbing from the relative security of his basket and inching backward along the keel toward the engine; he wore no safety harness, though the ground was more than 1,000 feet below. Traffic halted in the streets, and all Paris focused on the little figure tinkering with the engine as he clung like a high-wire artist to the insubstantial structure of his drifting dirigible. Soon the balky engine responded to Santos' ministrations with a steady chug, but precious time had been lost. Suspense mounted as the dirigible forged through the head wind toward St. Cloud, where the distinguished judges were observed jumping up and down with excitement. Santos drove his ship headlong over the starting line 29 minutes and 30 seconds after takeoff, but it took him another minute or so to land and thus stop the clock.

"Have I won?" he shouted, his eyes bright with triumph and excitement. "Tell me! Tell me!"

"Yes!" cried the crowd in unison, but of course the decision was not theirs to make.

Monsieur Deutsch pushed his way through the throng. "My own view is that you have won the prize," he told Santos in a voice hoarse with emotion. "But you are a few seconds over the time."

"My friend," confirmed the official timekeeper, "you have missed the prize by 40 seconds."

The enthusiastic crowd felt otherwise. "Give him the prize!" they yelled. *"Vive le petit Santos!"*

His face set, and looking suddenly far older than his 28 years, Santos turned his back on the judges, his airship and his vocal supporters, and drove home in an autumn drizzle.

For two weeks the dispute blazed in the newspapers, cafés and salons of Paris. In the end the Aero Club yielded to popular sentiment and declared Alberto Santos-Dumont winner of the Deutsch Prize; he donated 75,000 of the francs he received to the poor of Paris and divided

the rest among his own workmen. Brazil voted him an additional award of 125,000 francs, which he kept.

Santos continued to build airships over the next few years. The most successful of them was No. 9, a small, tubby and splendidly maneuverable craft. In this runabout he performed all manner of wonderful—and impudent—things. In 1903 a correspondent for the Paris weekly *L'Illustration* wrote of one such incident: "I had just sat down at the terrace of a café on the Avenue du Bois de Boulogne and was enjoying an iced orangeade. All of a sudden I was shaken with surprise on seeing an airship come right down in front of me. The guide rope coiled round the legs of my chair. The airship was just above my knees, and Monsieur Santos-Dumont got out. Whole crowds of people rushed forward and wildly acclaimed the great Brazilian aviator. He asked me to excuse him for having startled me. He then called for an apéritif, drank it down, got on board his airship again and went gliding off into space."

Such displays only faintly disguised Santos' growing inner disenchantment. "To propel a dirigible balloon through the air," he was heard to remark, "is like pushing a candle through a brick wall." He had developed his airships as far as his talents and vision allowed, but they never evolved beyond their role as personal vehicles for their inventor.

By 1905 Santos' interest had turned from airships to airplanes, and in 1906 he became the first man in Europe to achieve sustained flight in a heavier-than-air machine. But by 1910, when he was only 37, his health began to fail—his illness eventually was diagnosed as multiple sclerosis. He sank into a severe and lasting depression, sold his airship operation, paid off his workmen and went into a melancholy retirement. Returning finally to Brazil, he died in 1932 by his own hand—and was formally mourned by his country for three days.

Others in France had disputed Santos-Dumont's limited assessment of the dirigible's practicality. They envisioned much larger airships, capable of transporting goods and passengers across great distances. Two brothers, Paul and Pierre Lebaudy, owners of a sugar refinery near Mantes, constructed an ambitious airship of their own, Lebaudy I, in 1902. Designed by Henri Julliot, chief engineer at the Lebaudy sugar plant, the dirigible had a latticework of steel tubing attached to the bottom of the envelope, forming a keel. This semirigid construction made it possible to construct the Lebaudy I far larger than Santos' series of nonrigids, which had no internal structure at all. Propelled by a 40-horsepower Daimler engine, the Lebaudy I had a capacity of 80,000 cubic feet, could make 25 miles per hour in still air and remained steerable in a fresh breeze. These qualities were enough to attract the attention of the French military, which acquired Lebaudy I in 1905 and made it the prototype of a series of semirigid ships.

It was no simple matter to increase the dimensions—and thus the lifting power—of even a semirigid dirigible much beyond those of Julliot's design. The semirigids depended on a combination of gas pressure

The persistent Alberto Santos-Dumont takes off in his Airship No. 6 from St. Cloud, near Paris, on October 19, 1901. It was his fourth official attempt to win the Deutsch Prize, and this time he succeeded.

and the action of a ballonet to hold their shape. Larger ships required higher gas pressures, which in turn required stronger—and heavier—fabric for the ship's outer envelope. But this added weight would reduce the craft's load capacity and make it uneconomical to operate. What was needed to carry substantial loads was an entirely rigid airship that retained its shape even when empty of gas.

In 1851 a Frenchman, Prosper Meller, had conceived of such an airship built of iron, and in 1866 an Englishman, R. B. Boyman, patented a design for a rigid steel dirigible 1,320 feet long. Neither was ever built. Nor would either have succeeded. Both designs specified materials far too heavy for an airship.

The first rigid airship ever to be flown was built in the 1890s with a skeleton and outer cover made of an exotic new metal: aluminum. The new ship, designed by David Schwarz, a Dalmatian timber merchant, lifted off successfully in a tethered test in Berlin on November 3, 1897, but then had a stroke of bad luck. Its propeller belts broke. In an effort to

The French airship Clément-Bayard I is walked out of its hangar near Paris in 1908. Built by Henry Deutsch de la Meurthe's Astra Company, the nonrigid dirigible was distinguished by its gas-inflated stabilizing fins, which were lighter and easier to mount on the envelope than the usual narrow fins. But their bloated shape increased drag so much they were eventually abandoned.

retrieve the situation, the pilot valved gas—and bounced to a crash landing that destroyed the ship.

One man who was watching the demonstration closely that day came away determined that no such failure would ever be allowed to affect his plans. He too dreamed of a rigid airship, and his dream would finally bring the world into the dirigible era.

Count Ferdinand von Zeppelin was born in Württemberg, a small kingdom that became a satellite of Prussia; he was already 52 and a former brigadier of cavalry when he began seriously to consider building an airship in 1891. His motives were primarily martial, arising from the fear that the French would capitalize on the partially successful flight of *La France* seven years earlier to produce a fleet of military airships that would leave Prussia at a disadvantage in the event of war.

The Count had only one firsthand experience in the air. While in the United States in 1863 as the King of Württemberg's observer to the Union Army's prosecution of the Civil War, he had once gone up in a tethered observation balloon. A decade later his interest in flight was rekindled when he chanced to read a pamphlet by the German Postmaster General, Heinrich von Stephan, on the subject of "World Postal Service and Airship Travel."

"Providence has surrounded the entire earth with navigable air," Stephan had contended. "This vast ocean of air still lies empty today and wasted, and is not yet used for human transportation." The concept of a worldwide airship service tantalized the Count. During a period of hospitalization following a riding accident in 1874, he outlined plans— astonishing in their prescience—for a dirigible as big as an ocean liner, able to carry cargo, mail and 20 passengers. Most of the essential and distinguishing features of his future giant airships appeared in Zeppelin's sketches and notes: a rigid structure of vertical rings held in position by longitudinal girders, a row of separate gas cells between the rings, a fabric outer cover. But at that point in the 19th Century no suitable power plant existed. The Count was ahead of his time, and his ideas (like Santos-Dumont's) had to lie dormant until after the refinement of the internal-combustion engine.

As things turned out, the engine was only the first of the Count's problems. Though he had absorbed some technical knowledge after joining the Army at the age of 15, Zeppelin was not a trained engineer. His lack of expertise showed in the designs that he submitted to the Prussian War Ministry in his early attempts to secure government funds for his project.

Working out the technology as he went along, he initially proposed a sky train consisting of an airship locomotive towing two gas-filled freight cars, an idea that the War Ministry, not surprisingly, rejected out of hand. Zeppelin returned with a plan for a more conventional airship, which the War Ministry also turned down. The only alternative left was to raise the money he needed from private sources, and in 1898 he

Fully inflated with half a million cubic feet of illuminating gas, the envelope of John Morrell's airship, 485 feet long, looms over its handlers.

Fast fall for a sagging sausage

Innocent of any practical knowledge of airships, American inventor John Morrell set out to make aviation history in Berkeley, California, on May 23, 1908. At noon, Morrell, three photographers and a 16-man crew clambered on board the walkway lashed below an airship shaped like a giant sausage *(left)* and started its five automobile engines. Significantly, the man in charge of constructing the ship refused to join them.

The launch was uneven, some line handlers letting go before others. The single-celled ship—much too long for its own strength—staggered crookedly to an altitude of 300 feet *(above)*. The gas rushed to one end with such great pressure that the envelope burst, and as it fell *(right)*, men, engines and propellers were dumped into the watching crowd. Broken bones were abundant but, miraculously, no one was killed.

Hovering over the rooftops of Berkeley, the airship's muslin envelope begins to sag as the 20 men on board cling to its walkway.

Burst end first, Morrell's stricken airship crashes, climaxing the brief flight that one local newspaper account labeled "a monumental blunder from start to finish."

founded the Joint Stock Company for the Promotion of Airship Travel, with headquarters in Stuttgart. The company raised 800,000 marks, partly from public donations and partly from the Count's own fortune.

In June 1898 the construction of his first airship began at the village of Manzell, near Friedrichshafen, on Lake Constance, a place favored by consistently mild winds and weather. The airship was designated Luftschiff Zeppelin 1—LZ 1. When completed two years later it was a provocative piece of engineering. Four hundred twenty feet long and 38½ feet in diameter, LZ 1 had a capacity of 399,000 cubic feet. The lifting potential of that much hydrogen was more than 27,000 pounds, yet the airship, engines and ballast alone weighed so much that the craft could carry a payload of only 660 pounds when it took off on its first test flight on that July evening in 1900.

Had LZ 1 been able to lift a hundred times as much, the 18-minute flight for three and a half miles into the summer sunset would have been no less disappointing to close observers. Earlier airships had flown farther and faster and had been more maneuverable. The prestigious newspaper *Frankfurter Zeitung* commented the next day that the Count's experiments, while "extremely interesting, have undoubtedly proved conclusively that a dirigible balloon is of practically no value."

The Count remained optimistic. And indeed, the ship improved its performance substantially on subsequent flights that autumn, staying aloft for an hour and a half on its second ascent and doubling its speed to 17 miles per hour on the third. The Count had high hopes that the government would back him at last, but it did not. Now, having spent all the money he had raised, he had no option but to dismantle the airship, dismiss his workers and liquidate his company.

But Count von Zeppelin had not given up, and as evidence of that he retained his chief engineer, 22-year-old Ludwig Dürr. It was to prove one of the wisest decisions the frustrated crusader ever made.

The next few years were trying ones for the Count and his talented assistant. The German Army continued to have little use for the still-unproved invention as a long-range strategic scout or bomber. The Army was interested only in short-range tactical airships such as those the French were building, based on Julliot's Lebaudy I design. In 1903 the Count turned again to the public for funds. "I appeal to the German people," he wrote in a letter mailed to 60,000 Germans, "to sacrifice themselves for my undertaking and to support me in my persevering duty. Any sum will be welcome." But the public had lapsed into indifference and contributed only 8,000 marks. One member of the Union of German Engineers told the Count: "The monster will never rise again." However, the King of Württemberg, who had supported Zeppelin from the start, came to his rescue in 1904 by authorizing a kingdom-wide lottery that raised 124,000 marks. To get the rest of the money he needed to build a second airship, the Count mortgaged his wife's country estates in Latvia.

The sad destiny that awaited LZ 2 would have crushed a lesser man

Shy, brilliant Ludwig Dürr was 21 when he went to work for Count von Zeppelin in 1899. The next year he became chief engineer; his predecessor refused to fly in LZ 1 after Count von Zeppelin was unable to obtain insurance on the venture.

Its nose peeping out from a floating hangar (rear), the LZ 1 attracts an expectant crowd, including Queen Charlotte and King Wilhelm II of Württemberg (far left), before its third flight, in October 1900.

than Count von Zeppelin. No sooner was it paid for and built than it was destroyed. On a test flight in January 1906 both engines failed and the ship, driven helplessly before a stiff breeze, made a forced landing. Up to that point it was intact. But during the night high winds arose and battered the exposed ship into a wreck. The Count was desolate—at first. "I shall build no more airships," he said. But he soon changed his mind, and began work on a new ship, financed this time by the 250,000-mark proceeds from a Germany-wide lottery and a gift of 100,000 marks from the Prussian Kaiser himself, in recognition of Zeppelin's persistence.

Begun in May 1906, the LZ 3 was virtually identical to its most recent predecessor; it even used the two misbehaving engines salvaged from the wreck of LZ 2. The only significant difference was the addition of two pairs of horizontal stabilizer fins at the stern. Ludwig Dürr, Zeppelin's engineer, had prescribed the modification after tests in a crude wind tunnel indicated that the fins would help control the severe pitching the LZ 2 had experienced on its only flight.

The LZ 3 performed as if it were a child of a different father. On its first test flight it flew for two hours and 17 minutes, and achieved a speed of

Carrying members of the Reichstag on a sightseeing flight, a Zeppelin cruises over crowded Lake Constance in 1909 in this contemporary painting. The

lighthouse and sculpted lion at right mark the harbor entrance to Lindau.

24½ miles per hour while carrying 5,500 pounds of water ballast and 11 people. Its success revived the flagging enthusiasm of public and military alike, and the Count was awarded half a million marks to develop LZ 3 into a potential machine of war. If he could achieve a flight of 24 hours duration, the government promised to buy the airship. Zeppelin and Dürr spent the summer of 1907 on modifications—including the addition of horizontal tilting vanes fore and aft that converted the forward motion of the airship into lift for takeoffs with greater loads—and they took LZ 3 up on longer and longer flights over southern Germany. Once, the ship stayed nearly eight hours in the air and flew 220 miles.

Zeppelin developed sufficient confidence in LZ 3's reliability to allow various dignitaries—the King and Queen of Württemberg, the Crown Prince of Germany, the Count's own daughter, Countess Hella—to be taken up on pleasure trips. But it was clear that a 24-hour endurance flight was beyond the capacity of the craft; a bigger ship was needed to carry the necessary fuel and ballast. This time the government decided to put up the 400,000 marks needed to build LZ 4, which was similar to LZ 3 but bigger and better—able to lift more than half again as much. If the LZ 4 succeeded in staying airborne around the clock, the government promised to buy both LZ 3 and LZ 4 for 2.15 million marks.

The LZ 4 took off from the placid surface of Lake Constance shortly after sunrise on August 4, 1908, in an attempt to meet the endurance requirement. All the way up the Rhine valley, crowds congregated in the streets of the towns to watch the great ship growl past. Cannon were fired in salute from a castle battlement and spectators waved hats from the cathedral tower in Strasbourg. But the LZ 4 was destined never to return home.

An engine breakdown forced it to make an unscheduled landing in a field near Echterdingen, a small town southwest of Stuttgart. A great throng of curious people swarmed round the tethered craft, and soldiers had to be called out to guard it. While engineers from the nearby Daimler factory worked on the engine, the Count took a nap in one of the gondolas, then retired to a local inn. So the summer day passed, with the dirigible lying quietly, huge and incongruous, at the center of the congested meadow.

At three in the afternoon, while the mechanics were still at work, an unexpected squall came up and seized the ship, tearing its moorings from the ground. The soldiers strained in vain to hold the ship down, but it got away from them with a soldier and two crew members still on board. One crewman valved gas in an effort to bring the great hulk down again, but the bow brushed some trees, tearing the outer cover and apparently a gas cell as well. The cell was made of rubberized cloth; Count von Zeppelin and his engineers were not aware that when the fabric rubbed on itself it shot off sparks of static electricity. (Later cells would be made with an animal membrane that produced no sparks.)

There was a whoosh of flame, followed by a tremendous explosion. With other guests of the inn, Count von Zeppelin ran outside and

ZEPPELIN PURSE WITH THE COUNT'S PORTRAIT

HARMONICA WITH DECORATED CASE

Count von Zeppelin's elevation to the status of folk hero, triggered by the untimely destruction of the LZ 4 in 1908, inspired a profusion of mementos bearing the image of the Count and his airships.

ENAMELED GOLD CIGARETTE CASE

WOODEN NUTCRACKER

IVORY-TRIMMED BRUSH

looked on aghast as a towering fire consumed LZ 4. The destruction of the dirigible took just a few seconds. The soldier and the mechanics on board were miraculously spared.

With this disaster, even Count von Zeppelin was convinced that no airship of his would ever fly again. But he failed to appreciate how his stature had grown in the eyes of his countrymen. His determination and his limited successes had transformed him in public estimation from crazy inventor to national hero. Newspapers throughout the German Reich had eagerly followed his exploits. Sweetshops sold marzipan Zeppelins; tobacconists stocked Zeppelin cigarettes. Department stores offered Zeppelin yachting caps like the one worn by the 70-year-old Count; gardeners had named their prized blooms after him. City councilors had bestowed his name on squares, parks and streets, and official bodies of all kinds had heaped honors on the Count himself. Now, instead of recoiling in horror from the fiery demise of LZ 4, Germans rallied overwhelmingly to Zeppelin's support.

David Lloyd George, a British Cabinet member and future Prime Minister who was visiting Stuttgart, arrived at the scene of the fire shortly after it happened; he observed the beginning of what would become known as the "Miracle of Echterdingen." "Disappointment," he wrote in his memoirs, "was a totally inadequate word for the agony of grief and dismay which swept over the massed Germans who witnessed the catastrophe. The crowd swung into the chanting of 'Deutschland über Alles' with a fanatic fervor of patriotism."

Germans saw Count von Zeppelin and his airships as symbols of their aspirations as a nation; by the end of the day following the accident, citizens of the Reich had flooded the Count's headquarters with contributions to pay for a new airship. In the weeks that followed, funds continued to pour in—from the coffers of the Kaiser as well as from the piggy banks of children. Donations came not only from within Germany but from Germans living in other lands. Those who had no cash to give sent sausages, hams, wines and even hand-knitted woolen socks. Contributions from all sources totaled 6.25 million marks; suddenly Count von Zeppelin's airship scheme stood on a financial base firmer by far than ever before. "The desire of the German people to send forth airships built on my system to span the world," the Count wrote in a widely published thank-you letter to the nation, "will give me courage and the strength to continue my project." Thereafter he always referred to the Echterdingen disaster as his "glücklichste Unglücksfahrt" —his "luckiest unlucky trip."

The Count never looked back. He renovated his remaining ship, the LZ 3, and showed it off in November of 1908 to the Kaiser, who presented him with the Prussian Order of the Black Eagle. The government bought LZ 3 and gave it the Army designation Z I.

Count von Zeppelin and his dream were riding high, but new travail lay ahead. He used a portion of the more than six million marks he had received to organize the Zeppelin Airship Construction Company and began to build again in a new airship complex at Friedrichshafen. The German Army, over the objection of a number of skeptical officers, agreed in advance to purchase his next airship, LZ 5. In the spring of 1909 the LZ 5 made the longest voyage yet achieved in the brief history of powered flight—a triumphal 38-hour tour over the fatherland. Nevertheless, the skeptics were proved correct during trials later in the year when the new ship flew too slowly and too low to satisfy military standards. Consequently the generals refused to purchase LZ 6, which the Count's company had already built with a military sale in mind. Once more he was dangerously short of cash.

Count von Zeppelin had always regarded his airships as machines of war, but he realized that until the German Army came to share his opinion, he would have to find some other market for them. Reluctantly he agreed to the course recommended by his business manager, Alfred Colsman: He would start an airline.

Accordingly, the German Airship Transport Company (Deutsche Luftschiffahrts Aktien Gesellschaft, or DELAG for short) was established in 1909 to purchase Zeppelins, as the Count's rigid airships had come to be known, and to promote Zeppelin travel between major cities in Germany. The Hamburg-Amerika Line steamship company contracted its services as ticket agent, and several cities eager for airship service—Frankfurt, Baden Baden, Düsseldorf, Hamburg, Potsdam, Gotha, Leipzig and Dresden—offered hangars and landing space.

DELAG began operations in the summer of 1910; its first aircraft was a handsome new Zeppelin, LZ 7, christened the *Deutschland.* But the would-be airline might better have been named an airship-excursion company. During the next four years, its airships never managed to follow a schedule and did not fly at all during the winter. The slow craft simply were unable to overcome strong head winds. As a result, virtually all of the company's business came from taking passengers on two-hour tours of the countryside—with occasional extended excursions to other cities—on days when the winds promised to be light.

The inaugural flight of the *Deutschland,* on June 28, 1910, exemplified the problem. Carrying 23 journalists and a generous stock of caviar and champagne, the *Deutschland* headed downwind from Düsseldorf toward the scenic Wupper Valley. As a storm gathered, the wind on the Zeppelin's tail grew stronger and when the *Deutschland* turned for home it could make no headway at all, especially after one engine failed. On the contrary, the airship was blown backward into the storm and crash-landed in a forest. The airship did not catch fire and, except for a crewman who suffered a broken leg when he jumped from the rear gondola, there were no injuries.

Later that summer the LZ 6, which DELAG had begun using for passenger flights after the Army rejected it, burned in its shed from a fire started by workmen who were cleaning the gondolas with petrol. Less than a year later the fully loaded LZ 8, built to replace DELAG's first airship and named the *Deutschland II,* was picked up by a strong wind

Passengers escape the Deutschland II by ladder (right center) after a gusty crosswind smashed the airship onto its hangar and a windbreak fence at Düsseldorf in 1911. The captain, Hugo Eckener, vowed that never again would spectators and passengers pressure him into attempting a risky takeoff.

as it was walked out of its hangar. Despite the efforts of some 300 ground crewmen to restrain it, the ship got away and was impaled on a fence that had been erected as a windscreen to prevent such accidents. Again there was no fire and none of the passengers were injured.

Astonishingly, the public remained patient with DELAG, in spite of the fact that all three of the company's airships had either crashed or burned, having made fewer than 60 flights among them. Count von Zeppelin remained an immensely popular figure. The journalists who had been on board during the *Deutschland* accident reported on it in the most favorable terms possible, with high praise for a crew that was in fact virtually helpless. And the passengers on *Deutschland II,* because the airship never truly took off, probably never realized what a close brush they had with tragedy.

Such tolerance could not last forever. No one realized this more acutely than DELAG's Flight Director Hugo Eckener, who had commanded *Deutschland II* on its embarrassing and nearly disastrous encounter with the windscreen fence. Count von Zeppelin had recruited Eckener, a young political economist and part-time journalist, after Eckener had published technical articles critical of the Count's early dirigibles. In time, Eckener would become the most brilliant of Zeppelin captains and would inherit and expand the legacy of the Count himself. For now, he set about making the improvements in safety and reliability that were necessary if DELAG was to survive.

At Eckener's instigation, DELAG intensified the training of its crews, from commanding officers through helmsmen and mechanics, all of whom had perilously little experience handling their temperamental monsters in flight. The airline organized its own weather-forecasting network, with observation stations at each airship base. And to prevent a recurrence of the *Deutschland II* fiasco, at Eckener's suggestion the company installed docking rails to which an airship could be held fast against a wind by trolleys while it was moved from its hangar onto the field for takeoff and back to its berth after landing.

The Daimler engines had proved unreliable, so for its next ship, which was already under construction, DELAG turned to the Maybach Engine Manufacturing Company, organized two years earlier to make engines designed expressly for powering a rigid airship.

The first beneficiary of all this progress was the LZ 10, which made its first flight on June 26, 1911, and three weeks later was accepted by the airline. Slightly smaller and more maneuverable than either of the *Deutschlands,* the LZ 10 was christened the *Schwaben*—for Swabia, the ancient duchy in which Count von Zeppelin had been born. It turned out to be his, and DELAG's, lucky ship. Fitted with three 145-horsepower Maybach engines, the *Schwaben* reached a top speed of 47 miles per hour, and under Eckener's command it soon carried the flag to almost every corner of Germany.

To fly in the *Schwaben* was a treat to remember. Sitting at small tables near open windows, passengers dined on cold Westphalian ham and capon, paté from Strasbourg, Rhine wine and champagne served by a uniformed steward in a peaked cap. The fare charged was as patrician as the fare served: 200 marks for two hours, up to 600 marks for a longer trip. But price did not prevent the *Schwaben* from being an instant success—one couple even brought along their 16-week-old baby.

Over the next two years, DELAG augmented its fleet with three more commercial Zeppelins: the *Viktoria Luise* (named for the Kaiser's only daughter), the *Hansa* and the *Sachsen.* Germans by the thousands took to the air in what they regarded as the symbols of their national superiority in science and technology. Altogether, in four years of deluxe passenger service before World War I, DELAG's ships made 1,588 flights. They carried 10,197 fare-paying customers without inflicting so much as a bruise on any of them, although the *Schwaben*—one of the last airships to be built with rubberized gas cells instead of frictionproof material—was destroyed on the ground by fire in 1912 after one memorable year of service.

By this time, the Zeppelin Company had a competitor. Johann Schütte, a university professor of naval architecture, backed by an industrialist named Karl Lanz and other investors, organized a firm to manufacture rigid airships in Mannheim. The Schütte-Lanz ships, beau-

A DELAG poster in 1909 promises "Passenger Flights with Zeppelin Airships" over mapped routes, with tickets available at offices of the Hamburg-Amerika steamship line. Regular passenger schedules were never flown between cities, and the captains' choice of routes depended upon the direction of the wind.

Inside an opulent mahogany-paneled cabin decorated with a trimmed Christmas tree, passengers embark on a holiday flight in 1912. "Like streaks of mist," a company brochure promised, "anxiety and doubt will blow away."

tifully streamlined in comparison with the cylindrical Zeppelins, used laminated plywood instead of aluminum for their internal framework.

Public opinion brought the greatly improved performance of the rigid airships forcibly to the attention of the War Ministry, which gradually warmed to their potential for long-range reconnaissance and bombing. The Zeppelin had an influential military advocate in Count Helmuth von Moltke, Chief of the Army General Staff, and at his urging the Ministry began ordering airships in quantity. By 1914, six Zeppelins and one Schütte-Lanz had been stationed at key points along Germany's borders. The Navy took somewhat longer to be persuaded, however, and the Navy Minister, Admiral Alfred von Tirpitz, was especially skeptical. "The thing itself is not very safe," he had noted after the LZ 4 burned at Echterdingen. "Whether the concept is safe is very much in dispute." But in 1912, bowing to pressure from the Kaiser and to disquieting news that the navies of other nations were developing airships, he placed an order for the Navy's first Zeppelin.

The aging Count was overjoyed at the change in the military's attitude. After struggling more than 20 years, he had lived to see his first and fondest dream for his creations about to come true: Instead of passengers, Zeppelins would carry bombs in their bellies. ➤➤

A time of gentle giants

During the four years after the airship line DELAG began carrying passengers in 1910, the creations of Count Ferdinand von Zeppelin became a common part of Germany's tranquil airscape. Their random flights thrilled the venturous thousands who took them and aroused patriotic admiration in thousands more who merely watched. But their commercial nature frustrated the Count, who was obsessed with the need for military preparedness.

Still, the Count continued to produce new airships, each one more reliable than the last, and their excursions doubled as training missions for scores of military aircrews. When war came, Germany had a unique military asset—just as Count von Zeppelin had intended—thanks to the carefree flights of the gentle DELAG giants.

The LZ 6, which became one of DELAG's first passenger ships, attracts a flotilla of curious boaters as it is moved tail first out of its floating hangar on Lake Constance.

DELAG's first unqualified success, the LZ 10, named the Schwaben, takes off from Friedrichshafen in 1911 without disturbing the grazing sheep that helped keep the airfield's grass trimmed.

49

2

Wartime missions for nocturnal monsters

When the British went to war against Germany on August 4, 1914, they fully anticipated that the skies over England would soon be aswarm with giant Zeppelin bombers. The German public enjoyed similar expectations; even the school children favored a lusty song that urged the mighty airships to fly against the enemy. "England," they sang, "will be destroyed by fire."

In fact, Germany was ill-prepared to mount such an onslaught. DELAG's small commercial fleet was conscripted for military duty. But the Navy had lost two of its three airships—along with most of its seasoned crewmen—in peacetime accidents, and four of the Army's six Zeppelins were brought down by hostile ground fire during the first weeks of warfare. Count von Zeppelin's company lacked the production facilities to quickly replenish this diminished armada; in any case, Kaiser Wilhelm, bound by blood ties to the British Royal Family, was reluctant to authorize air strikes against his kinsmen's homeland.

All this was to change drastically, owing largely to the passionate faith and ruthless dynamism of a single officer: Commander Peter Strasser. Born in 1876 and a lifelong bachelor, Strasser was a dedicated professional Navy man who had volunteered for aviation duty as early as 1911. He had become Chief of the Naval Airship Division in 1913, following the death of his predecessor in an airship crash at sea. A hard taskmaster and a stickler for discipline, Strasser soon forged his rigid dirigibles into one of the most dramatic new weapons of the Great War. Four months after the outbreak of hostilities, 25 Navy flight crews were in training or were already in service; a total of 3,740 officers and men were stationed at nine bases, most of which were located along the north German coast.

The Zeppelin Company responded to the challenge of war by agreeing to build 26 military airships, of an enlarged and improved design, by 1915. The company also launched a far-reaching research and development program that would lead to a virtual German monopoly on rigid military airships. The eight British rigids that flew during the War were technically about five years behind the German models and had little impact on the conflict. And the French showed scant interest in rigid

Probing lights isolate two German Zeppelins above the Houses of Parliament in this watercolor of a bombing raid on London in 1915, the year in which airships came of age as weapons of war.

airships, confining their activities to relatively small semirigid and nonrigid dirigibles.

Germany's Army, not to be outdone by the Navy, expanded its airship service too, although—lacking a Strasser—it would never match the Navy's in size or effectiveness. Adding to its prewar sites, the Army established airship bases on the Western Front, as well as along the Eastern Front from the Baltic to the Balkans.

It was the Navy, whose warships for the most part were bottled up by a British blockade, that would take the lead in mounting the Zeppelin's most spectacular and damaging effort of the War: a strategic bombing campaign against Britain. "We dare not leave any means untried of forcing England to her knees," wrote the naval staff's deputy chief in October 1914, and within a few months the means were at hand; all that was needed was word from the Kaiser.

That word came on January 10, 1915, in a telegram to the commander of the German fleet: "Air attacks on England approved by the Supreme War Lord." The momentous directive was limited, however, and the raiders were authorized to bomb only docks and military facilities on the lower Thames or on the coast. London was not to be a target.

Strasser and his eager Zeppelin commanders were quick to act. On January 13, a four-ship raiding squadron set out across the North Sea for England, bearing a cargo of explosive and incendiary bombs. This first assault was turned back by bad weather, but six days later three of the raiders tried again. The ship carrying Strasser suffered engine trouble and returned to its base at Nordholz, but the remaining two droned on to the English coast, where their bombs damaged the town square at Yarmouth, destroyed some small houses and killed four people. History's first campaign to pound a nation into submission from the air had begun. And while German airships would attack cities in other countries—among them Belgium, France, Poland, Rumania and Russia—England would bear the brunt of the War's aerial bombardment.

All Zeppelin raids on Britain would follow the same general plan. Timing was important, and restrictive. The raids were always made at night and almost always during the dark of the moon—the period extending from eight days before the new moon to eight days after—when the huge airships were least visible to the enemy's fighter planes and ground fire. The ships would take off from their bases in late morning or early afternoon and make their landfall over the English coast at dusk. They would arrive over their targets during the darkest hours and be well on their way back to Germany before dawn. Raids were seldom staged in midsummer, when nights were not long enough or dark enough to provide the necessary cover, or in winter, when weather conditions made for hazardous flying.

Under the circumstances, conventional naviation was extremely difficult. The darkness was frequently compounded by clouds and, later in the War, by the blackout of English towns, making visual orientation

Commander Peter Strasser, the head of Germany's Naval Airship Division, was a stern disciplinarian capable of issuing "black cigars"—German Navy slang for salty tongue-lashings—but he was revered for his concern for his men's welfare and his willingness to share their dangers.

impossible. Errors of drift, caused by the inability to measure the strength and direction of the wind, complicated the problem, leading to wild mistakes in estimates of position plotted by dead reckoning.

When Zeppelins L 5, L 6 and L 7 went raiding on April 15, 1915, none of their captains had the slightest idea where over England they were. One of them at least stumbled on a novel way to determine where he had been. The commander of the L 6 was Lieutenant Horst Treusch von Buttlar-Brandenfels, a dashing 26-year-old Hessian baron. Steering his 518-foot ship toward what appeared to be the lights of an English city, Buttlar was caught by searchlights and hit by ground fire that riddled three of the ship's gas cells. He jettisoned his bombs and ran for home. The next morning, safely on the ground at his airship base near Hamburg, he reported by telephone to his chief, Commander Strasser.

Asked to name the town he had bombed, Buttlar stammered that opinions were still divided as to the precise spot, but that he would pinpoint the target in his official report. Later that day, while he was relaxing in an alehouse and wondering how he would live up to his promise, the airshipman bought an evening paper that carried a sketchy announcement of the previous night's raid. It included an extract from a Dutch newspaper report that a German airship had bombarded the English town of Maldon.

Buttlar dashed to the telephone and called the clerk who was preparing his report. "Write Maldon in the space left for the name of the place raided," he said, "and send copies off by express messenger at once."

Later Buttlar heard from his superiors: "The accurate navigation of the airship and location of the place raided," they said, "were worthy of the highest praise."

At the beginning of May 1915, German airshipmen were assigned a target that they would have little trouble finding. After vacillating for months, the Kaiser gave permission for the bombing of London—though he restricted the attacks to military and strategic targets outside the heart of the city. On fine nights early in the War the lights of the capital of the British Empire glowed on the horizon like an aurora—visible for miles from the gondola of a Zeppelin.

An Army airship piloted by Captain Erich Linnarz had the distinction of dropping the first bombs on London. Linnarz steered his ship, the LZ 38, over the unsuspecting city on the night of May 31, 1915. "London was all lit up and we enjoyed total surprise," he wrote in his report. "Not a searchlight or an antiaircraft gun was aimed at us before the first bomb was dropped." Linnarz was over his target for a little more than 10 minutes. He released nearly all of his 154 bombs, killing seven civilians and injuring 35. The bombs also started 41 fires and caused substantial property damage.

Linnarz was not so successful a week later. Soon after taking off for England, in tandem with the LZ 37, his ship began to experience engine trouble and returned to its base—where the very next morning it was destroyed on the ground by two British Navy aircraft. The LZ 37 suf-

Tense hours on board a raider

For reasons of security few photographic records were made of operations on board World War I military dirigibles, but artists were on hand to fill the need. A German illustrator named Felix Schwormstädt did a unique series of sketches and watercolors that caught all the drama of a bombing mission, although he never went on one.

Working from the recollections of the crew of airship LZ 38, Schwormstädt in 1917 achieved a highly realistic reconstruction of a raid that had taken place over England two years earlier. His art recaptures vividly the tension experienced by an airship crew over hostile territory: the strain in the tiny (six-and-a-half-by-nine-foot) control gondola, where the captain, executive officer, rudder operator and elevator helmsman navigated the great dirigible; the concentration required of mechanics who had to maintain and repair engines in the middle of combat; and—most striking—the desperate courage of gunners and observers compelled to do their difficult work from outside the skin of the airship.

In LZ 38's control gondola Captain Erich Linnarz reaches for a speaking tube connected to the bomb room amidships. From the left, an officer keeps watch while the elevator and rudder operators maintain the ship's altitude and course, and a mechanic climbs down from the hull.

A machine gunner and an observer fight off British planes from their perilous post atop the hull. Later airships were equipped with a second gun platform at the stern.

In the LZ 38's rear gondola a machine gunner with a 30-caliber Parabellum cranes for a glimpse of enemy aircraft while mechanics work on one of the Zeppelin's four 210-hp Maybach C-X engines.

fered an even worse fate. Flying over Belgium on its way to London, the Zeppelin was attacked from above and bombed into a flaming mass by a lone British pilot, Sublieutenant Reginald A. J. Warneford, flying a Morane-Saulnier monoplane. The LZ 37's ten crewmen had no parachutes, which would have added cumbersome weight to the lighter-than-air craft, and all but one of them perished with their ship. The lucky survivor was saved when the impact of the crashing control car threw him through the roof of a convent and into a recently vacated bed.

The loss of the LZ 37 cast a momentary pall over the airshipmen of Germany but did little to check the military leadership's appetite for airship operations. Though the Army's two ships on the Western Front were transferred to the east, the Navy stepped up the pace of its activities. The Naval Airship Division soon had 18 ships, and an order was placed with the Zeppelin Company for a new two-million-cubic-foot supership. Air-minded admirals and generals were confident that airships could cripple the British war effort by destroying commerce and industry and by crushing the will of the civilian populace.

After a two-month pause in midsummer, Commander Strasser's air fleet resumed its onslaught with a vengeance. London was now the priority target. Abolishing his previous restrictions, the Kaiser had agreed to an all-out campaign to smash the commercial heart of the British Empire; only palaces and historic buildings were to be spared.

In August 1915, as the nights began to lengthen, Strasser dispatched several sorties of four or five airships each, but engine breakdowns, faulty navigation and bad weather kept all but one Zeppelin from reaching London. That ship's commander claimed that he bombed the central city, though his bombs actually fell in the northeastern suburbs, killing 10 civilians and wounding 48 more. But this attack was merely a prelude to a raid that would strike at the heart of London.

Just after two on the afternoon of September 8, 1915, Lieutenant Commander Heinrich Mathy gave a terse order from the forward control car of the Navy Zeppelin L 13. "Airship up!" The ground crewmen released their grip on the handrails attached to the gondolas—the last restraint on the free-floating airship. Slowly it moved forward and upward over the north German coastal air base at Hage. When the ship had reached 1,000 feet the engineers set the four finely tuned Maybach C-X engines at cruising speed and Mathy ordered his rudderman to steer toward Norderney, an island in the North Sea; there he rendezvoused with three other raiders—the L 9, L 11 and L 14—and set a westerly course. The L 13, its bomb bay loaded with nearly 4,000 pounds of explosive and incendiary missiles, was bound for London.

The ship droned steadily through the long afternoon, its bow rising and falling slowly in the buffeting air currents. The 16 officers and men settled into their flight routine: Lookouts stationed in the gondolas and on top of the airship scanned the sea for enemy warships; in each of the engine gondolas a crew member stood by to detect malfunctions in

Hopelessly aflame, Germany's LZ 37, in June 1915, becomes the first dirigible ever to be destroyed in air-to-air combat. Its conqueror, a Morane monoplane flown by British Sublieutenant R. A. J. Warneford, veers to avoid the inferno.

the Zeppelin's power plants. Those who were not on duty rested in hammocks slung along the gangway inside the hull, between the forward and after gondolas.

The L 13 raised the English coast at 8:35 p.m., but Mathy hovered offshore for an hour to await total darkness before heading inland. The L 9 had long since peeled off from the other three airships and headed for its assigned target—a chemical plant in the north of England; the L 11 and L 14 were experiencing engine trouble that would prevent them from reaching London. Mathy's airship alone would bomb the British capital that night.

Shrouded by the black night, the Zeppelin moved inland at an altitude of nearly 7,000 feet. Mathy, peering earthward from his station in the control car, was guided by the rivers and well-lighted villages below until he reached Cambridge, some 60 miles north of his goal. From there, he simply steered for the brilliant glow of lights on the horizon.

By 11:30 p.m. the L 13 was passing over the northwestern suburbs of London. All was quiet in the control car now, the silence broken only by quick commands to the helmsman. Mathy had spent a week in London in 1909, and he had little trouble making out the prominent features of the enemy city spread below him. The Inner Circle of Regent's Park, he wrote later, was "lit as in peacetime."

London's peace was soon shattered. "Fire slowly," Mathy ordered his bombardier, and a mixture of high explosives and incendiaries began to fall. The first bombs hit a residential quarter near the British Museum; others dropped in widely spaced bunches as Mathy steered toward the looming bulk of St. Paul's Cathedral on a course calculated to bring him over his main objective, the Bank of England.

For the first time in history, the civilian population of a huge metropolis was experiencing the fury of 20th Century aerial bombardment. An American journalist, W. E. Shepherd, watched the raid from Fleet Street and wrote of the unprecedented scene around him:

"Traffic is at a standstill. A million quiet cries make a subdued roar. People stand gazing into the sky from the darkened streets. Among the autumn stars floats a long, gaunt Zeppelin. It is dull yellow—the color of the harvest moon. The long fingers of searchlights, reaching up from the roof of the city, are touching all sides of the death messenger with their white tips. Great booming sounds shake the city. They are Zeppelin bombs—falling—killing—burning. Lesser noises, of shooting, are nearer at hand, the noise of aerial guns sending shrapnel into the sky.

" 'For God's sake, don't do that!' says one man to another, who has just struck a match to light a cigarette.

"Whispers, low voices, run all through the streets.

"Suddenly you realize that the biggest city in the world has become the night battlefield on which seven million harmless men, women and children live."

For the 16 men in the marauding airship, the sky too had become a battlefield. Gripped by the British searchlights, the L 13 was brilliantly exposed to the gunners below. The crewmen could see the flicker of antiaircraft fire far beneath them; much nearer the ship, they saw the red flashes of exploding shrapnel and the blue-white trails of deadly incendiary shells.

Mathy knew, as he said later, that at any minute his ship might be "plunged below in a shapeless mass of wreckage and human bodies dashed unrecognizable." But he pressed on. The L 13 carried a 660-pound high-explosive bomb, the largest yet taken on a raid over England. Mathy evidently hoped to drop this blockbuster on the Bank of England. But he had miscalculated his position; when released, the bomb fell relatively harmlessly near an ancient church. Looking down from the control car, Mathy was nonetheless impressed with the destructive effect of his giant bomb: "A whole cluster of lights," he noted, "vanished in its crater."

By now the British gunners were coming close to their quarry, and Mathy ordered the L 13 to climb from 8,500 feet to 11,200, where he found cover behind a thin cloud bank. He still had a few bombs left, and

Lieutenant Commander Heinrich Mathy, regarded by friend and foe as the War's premier airship captain, keeps watch from the control gondola of L 13.

he ordered them dropped over the Liverpool Street railroad station. "There was a succession of detonations and bursts of fire," he said later. "I could see that I had hit well and had apparently done great damage." In fact, he had destroyed a few feet of railway track and scored direct hits on two buses, killing 15 people.

The L 13 began its long journey back to Germany, a nine-hour flight across the North Sea. In the control car, Mathy began writing his mission report; crewmen who could be spared from duty dozed fitfully in their hammocks. On the ground behind them, British fire fighters labored to quench the flames still raging in the textile warehouses along the crooked lanes near St. Paul's Cathedral. When Londoners finished assessing the damage left in the wake of Heinrich Mathy's solo attack, they found that the L 13 in only 15 minutes of bombardment had killed 32 people and had caused property damage amounting to a staggering £530,787 (about $2.5 million).

Mathy tried to repeat his London mission five days later, but he turned back when his Zeppelin was damaged by a coastal antiaircraft battery. He came again on October 13, 1915, leading a squadron of five airships against the British capital. However, this time his navigation was faulty and, along with all but one of the other raiders, he failed to reach his intended target.

The exception was Lieutenant Commander Joachim Breithaupt, piloting the L 15 in his first flight to England. Breithaupt held a steady course for central London, and at 10 p.m. his ship appeared over the Houses of Parliament. A late-night debate was in session in the House of Commons and, as the sounds of antiaircraft fire came through the open windows, a low cry of "Zeppelins! Zeppelins!" spread through the chamber. Members rushed outside to investigate.

"There she is!" cried one man, pointing excitedly into the cloudless, starlit sky. A reporter on the scene recalled that the airship "was then played upon by two searchlights, and in their radiance she looked a thing of silvery beauty sailing serenely through the night, indifferent to the big gun roaring at her from the Green Park, whose shells seemed to burst just below her."

As his ship flew over Charing Cross Station, Breithaupt ordered his bombs released. He wrote later of the curiously enchanting spectacle that greeted him: "London lies below us almost dark. Before us lies a broad, well-aimed barrage of bursting shells, brightly illuminated by searchlights. It is an unforgettable picture, this bursting of shrapnel, and below, the crashing of bombs and the roar of guns."

Breithaupt's primary targets had been the Bank of England and the Admiralty, headquarters of the British Navy, but his first bombs fell instead in the teeming theater district. In one street 17 people were killed by a single bomb, but hotels and crowded theaters miraculously escaped destruction. Some playgoers heard the bombs exploding but were advised to remain inside rather than rush into the streets. At the Gaiety Theatre, an American musical comedy called *Tonight's the*

Night continued without a break after one of the cast turned to the audience and said in a stage whisper: "Gun practice."

Outside, bodies lay on the pavement and in shop doorways. A shattered bus smoldered near the Waldorf Hotel. Jets of flame erupted from a broken gas main, and curious crowds were forced back by the police as stretcher-bearers carried off the wounded.

Breithaupt was not unopposed as he moved over London—ever since his approach to the city, the British crew of a French 75mm mobile gun had been racing through the streets to get into firing position. Its first shot burst below the airship and took Breithaupt by surprise; the second exploded dangerously close. Then a new threat appeared—four British airplanes had risen to pursue the German intruder. Breithaupt wrote in his combat report that the planes "were clearly recognizable in the searchlight illumination and by their exhaust flames." But only one of the British planes spotted the giant shape of the L 15, and Breithaupt was able to climb safely out of its range before turning for home. The German raiders had done effective work. Breithaupt and his fellow commanders, who had dropped their bombloads on other parts of England, left behind 71 dead and 128 injured in the smoking ruins.

Although the coming of stormy winter weather sharply reduced air activity—months passed before another squadron-scale raid took place—Germany's high command was more determined than ever to press an aerial campaign that would force England to sue for peace. And the British were just as determined to defend their island.

At the end of May 1916, the German Naval Airship Division took delivery of the airship L 30, the first of the radically improved, two-million-cubic-foot super Zeppelins that had been ordered the previous year. The giant was 650 feet long and 90 feet high; six engines gave it a maximum speed of 62 miles per hour. It carried 10 machine guns, could reach a ceiling of 13,000 feet with combat load and had a maximum lift of 141,200 pounds—including five tons of bombs.

Strasser had high hopes for this new breed of Zeppelin. "The performance of the big airships has reinforced my conviction that England can be overcome by airships," he wrote, "inasmuch as the country will be deprived of the means of existence through increasingly extensive destruction of cities, factory complexes, railroads, dockyards, harbor works with warships and merchant ships lying therein." The airships, he concluded, "offer a certain means of victoriously ending the War."

Strasser launched his first major assault of the autumn raiding season on August 24, sending 13 airships on a bombing run against England. British Navy vessels, alerted to the attack by German radio signals, fired upon at least six of the raiders, sending one back to its base with a punctured gas cell. But the weather did more than gunfire did to stop the marauding airships. Five of them were turned back by head winds before reaching the coast; most of the others were kept from their targets by clouds, engine failure and navigational errors. Only one of the

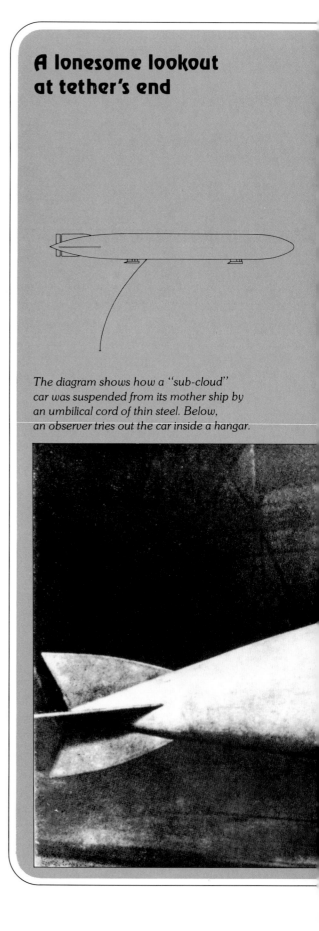

A lonesome lookout at tether's end

The diagram shows how a "sub-cloud" car was suspended from its mother ship by an umbilical cord of thin steel. Below, an observer tries out the car inside a hangar.

"There I hung, exactly as if I had been in a bucket, down a well," said a German airshipman, describing one of the War's loneliest assignments: as observer in a "sub-cloud" car *(below)*. Lowered by winch from its mother ship, the tiny duralumin car dangled at the end of a steel cable as much as a half mile long *(left)*. The observer served as a human periscope: While the airship stayed hidden above the clouds, he called in bomb strikes by telephone from below them.

Germany's two airship services were divided on the cars' value: The Army outfitted many of its Zeppelins with the half-ton units, but the Navy rejected them as "useless weight." Crew members were also equivocal. One man complained that he felt like a "disembodied spirit floating about in space." Some, however, relished the chance to drift far below the hydrogen-filled mother ship and enjoy a pastime that was strictly *verboten* above—smoking a cigarette.

raiders, a new supership under Heinrich Mathy's command, got through to London, where its bombs hit a power station, killed nine civilians and injured 40 more.

A little more than a week later, on September 2, 1916, Strasser made another show of strength, dispatching 12 of his airships to London in company with four ships from the Army. It was the largest air armada yet assembled, but it would not come back unscathed.

The first German raider to approach the British capital was the Army ship LZ 98, commanded by Lieutenant Ernst A. Lehmann. As it dropped its bombs and came under fire from the ground at Gravesend, 20 miles east of London, the LZ 98 was pursued by Second Lieutenant William Leefe Robinson, a 21-year-old Royal Flying Corps pilot who was patrolling the night skies in a black-painted biplane, his machine gun armed with recently developed explosive bullets. Lehmann managed to slip away in the clouds, and Robinson, deprived of one quarry, set out in search of another.

At the same time, another Army airship was bearing down on London from the north. It was the SL 11, newly launched in Leipzig by Zeppelin's competitor, the Schütte-Lanz Company. Its commander, the London-born Captain Wilhelm Schramm, began dropping his bombload when he reached the outskirts of the city, but was soon forced to turn back by heavy ground fire. He was heading northeast, the air around him alive with bursting shells and tracer bullets, when Robinson appeared overhead. The young pilot put his plane into a dive, dropped below the lumbering airship and laced it from one end to the other with his explosive bullets. Schramm's SL 11 continued flying with no apparent damage, even after Robinson swooped alongside to rake the ship with another long burst. Trying yet another tack, Robinson dropped slightly below and behind the retreating German airship and this time concentrated his fire, loosing an entire drum of ammunition at a single section of its hull.

Suddenly the rear of the airship began to glow. Almost at once the fire spread through the whole of the hydrogen-filled craft. Engulfed in flames, the SL 11 seemed to hang motionless for a moment, then it began to fall slowly, almost majestically, to earth.

Other German airshipmen, still converging on London, watched in horror as the blazing SL 11 lighted up the sky. On board the LZ 98, which earlier had escaped from Robinson, Ernst Lehmann heard his first officer let out a wild cry; he turned to see a great ball of fire, like a blazing meteor, on the far side of London. And from 50 miles away, the commander of another ship, the L 11, made this entry in his war diary: "Enormous flame over London, slowly sinking below cloud horizon, gradually diminishing. Burning airship." Six of the remaining German commanders abandoned the attack and ran for home, shaken by the disaster they had witnessed and depressed by its dreadful portent.

A million Londoners reacted quite differently. As the SL 11 flamed in the sky, the crowds below cheered. Railway locomotives whistled in salute and men and women danced in the streets. From Windsor to the mouth of the Thames, the English came out to watch the end of the first German airship brought down in flames over England. They saw the ball of fire swell and then burst in an explosion of intense white incandescence. Then the ship's nose dipped and it began a flaming dive from 12,000 feet. In one crowd of spectators, someone started to sing the anthem "Land of Hope and Glory." "It was taken up one after another by the people that were congregated there," recalled an onlooker, "until the whole place seemed to be resonant with this singing."

The SL 11 fell toward Cuffley, north of London, and as it neared the ground and began to disintegrate, the villagers could hear the crackling of the fire and feel the intense heat on their faces. With a loud crunch the ship crashed in a field behind a pub. Its ammunition exploding like firecrackers, the SL 11 burned for two hours until there was almost nothing of it left—unlike the Zeppelins, the Schütte-Lanz ships had frameworks of wood instead of aluminum. Few of the 16 crew members were recognizable as human beings, though one charred body was found with a hand clutching part of the ship's rudder wheel.

The destruction of the SL 11 lifted British morale and correspondingly depressed the Germans. The German Army, unwilling to risk further losses, sent no more airships against England. But Strasser and his Navy airshipmen were not so easily discouraged.

The next attacks began three weeks later, on September 23, when a dozen Navy raiders set off for England. Eight older-type Zeppelins aimed for the Midlands; the remaining four ships, all new super Zeppelins under Mathy's overall command, headed for London. The L 30, captained by Horst von Buttlar, had navigation problems and never reached its target. The others, L 31, L 32 and L 33, found their way to the British capital.

Mathy, in the control car of the L 31, had lost none of his boldness and enterprise. Using parachute flares to blind the ground batteries and to check his position from time to time, he homed in on the now-blacked-out city by following railroad tracks and achieved surprise by attacking from the city's weakly defended southern edge; his bombing run carried him straight across London and he escaped toward the northeast. It was the first time an airship had traversed London, yet Mathy's bombs somehow missed the center city; the damage and casualties were limited to residential areas. Mathy slipped away from London above a thick ground mist.

His fellow captains were not as fortunate. Lieutenant Commander Alois Böcker of the L 33, making its maiden raid, shared Mathy's daring but lacked his finesse. He struck boldly along the most direct route to London, blinding the gunners on the ground with dazzling magnesium flares dropped by parachute. He came in over the populous East End, where his bombs set off huge fires in a lumberyard and an oil depot. Thirty searchlights probed for him, and at 13,000 feet he was within range of the artillery barrage that followed. One shell hit home, bursting

A British recruiting poster decries the bombing of women and children by German airships. The raids so galvanized the citizens of the once-secure island that one of the German airship crewmen said he felt as if he had become "a recruiting officer for the British Army."

inside a gas cell and riddling a number of other cells with fragments. The L 33 began to lose hydrogen at a prodigious rate; it did not catch fire, but the ship began to sink at 800 feet a minute. Böcker coaxed his stricken craft toward the sea for the long run home, while crewmen inside the hull worked feverishly to patch the holes. A British fighter plane intercepted the slow-moving airship and raked it with bullets until the pilot's machine gun jammed.

The L 33 staggered on. Desperately, the crew jettisoned everything that could be spared to lighten the ship—boots and clothing, guns and ammunition boxes, tools and reserve fuel. But hydrogen continued to pour out of the riddled gas cells and the ship continued to lose altitude.

Böcker realized the L 33 could never reach Germany. His only hope now was to put down in the sea close enough to shore for the crew to scramble to safety. The L 33, its nose pointed sharply skyward, had only 500 feet of altitude left as it approached the Essex coast. There, it was caught by a draft and forced down in a farm field near the village of Little Wigborough. All 22 crew members climbed out unhurt. Böcker set out to destroy his ship. He heaped the ship's papers in the control car, then stood back and fired a signal flare into a puddle of gasoline in the gangway. A blast of exploding hydrogen from one of the punctured gas cells knocked the survivors down. Soon the Zeppelin was reduced to a skeleton of red-hot girders glowing in the dark.

The men of the L 33 fell in and marched off down a country lane—the only armed Germans to march across English soil in World War I. Böcker had a faint hope of finding a boat and sailing home across the North Sea, but his presence was hardly a secret, and as his little band headed down the lane they were followed, at a distance, by a growing crowd of villagers. Eventually they were confronted by a lone English bobby on a bicycle.

"Can you tell me," asked Böcker coolly, "how far we are from Colchester?"

"Never mind about Colchester," the policeman replied. "You come along with me." And so, shuffling obediently behind the bobby as he pedaled his wobbly bike, the crew of the L 33 proceeded into captivity.

At almost the same hour that the L 33 crash-landed in Essex, its sister ship L 32 also came to rest on English soil—under disastrous circumstances. This 650-foot super Zeppelin was commanded by one of the Navy's ablest airship captains, Lieutenant Werner Peterson, who was on his 11th mission over England. Dazzled by the London searchlights and harassed by ground fire, Peterson was trying to gain altitude and make his getaway when his ship was pounced on by a British fighter plane. The pilot, Second Lieutenant Frederick Sowrey, sprayed a mixture of explosive, incendiary and tracer bullets down the length of the L 32. The first two drums of ammunition had no visible effect on the huge target, so Sowrey decided to concentrate all of the third drum on a single section, amidships. He had fired 30 rounds when he saw a light inside the hull; in a matter of seconds the light had spread until it engulfed the entire ship. Sowrey put his plane into a steep, turning dive to avoid the fiery mass as it went past him, roaring and crackling. The fire was so bright that crew members of a British submarine on the surface in the Straits of Dover, 60 miles away, clearly saw the glow.

The L 32 crashed in a beet field near the village of Billericay. Though it continued to burn for nearly an hour, some items—the crew's intended breakfast of bacon, black bread and potatoes, Peterson's gray greatcoat, and the priceless new secret signal book of the German Navy—survived the flames. Only one of the crew had jumped; his body was found nearby. The remaining 21 crewmen had stayed with their ship and were burned beyond recognition.

The vision of death by fire had begun to haunt the men of the Naval Airship Division. They continued to fly, however, and their missions became increasingly dangerous. On September 25, just two days after the costly London attack, Mathy made an assault on the heavily defended Royal Navy base at Portsmouth. His bombs did no harm.

A week later, on October 1, Mathy set off yet again for England with a squadron of 11 Zeppelins. The raiders ran into bad weather, and most of them drifted aimlessly over the darkened English countryside. Three commanders turned back without dropping their bombs. But Mathy, resourceful as ever, maintained a steady course to London in the L 31. He was probing the city's outer defenses and was under heavy fire from ground batteries when four British pilots spotted his ship.

Mathy saw the planes coming. He dropped all his bombs and began to climb, making a sharp turn to the west as he did so. But one of the planes, flown by Second Lieutenant Wulstan J. Tempest, dived from 16,500 feet, overtook the fleeing Zeppelin and opened fire. The Germans fought back with their own machine guns, but Tempest eluded their fire and continued to pump incendiary bullets into the L 31's hull. Suddenly Tempest saw the ship "begin to go red inside like an enormous Chinese lantern." Flames poured from the nose of the Zeppelin, which shot upward for about 200 feet, then went into a death plunge. The L 31 crashed in a pasture not far from Cuffley, where the SL 11 had fallen in flames a month earlier.

In a corner of the field, villagers found Lieutenant Commander Mathy, heavily clad in uniform and greatcoat, with a thick muffler tied around his neck. He had jumped from his burning ship long before it struck the ground, and had landed so heavily that the imprint of his body was visible in the stubbly grass. Somehow still alive when they found him, Mathy died soon afterward in the arms of a villager.

The death of their foremost bomber captain was shattering to Germany's airshipmen, and their growing sense of despair was heightened by the loss of two more Zeppelins—both brought down in flames by British fighter pilots. The German Army decided to disband its airship service in favor of long-range airplanes such as the twin-engined Gothas

British sentinels guard the remains of the downed German airship L 31 in October of 1916. The disaster had taken the life of Germany's most successful airship captain, Heinrich Mathy.

and four-engined Giants (built by the Zeppelin Company) that were soon to be launched on a new kind of bombing campaign against England. The Navy, too, seemed to be on its way out of the airship war. Replacing Zeppelins was relatively slow and very expensive, and at the prevailing loss rate the Navy within a few months would have none left.

But the single-minded Peter Strasser, who enjoyed the complete confidence of the fleet commander, Vice Admiral Reinhard Scheer, kept faith with his airships, continued to argue forcefully in defense of airships as bombers. He conceded that the damage they caused might be slight in terms of the total war effort, but he maintained that their psychological effect on the civilian population—coupled with the diversionary value of tying up men, planes and guns—more than justified their continued use over England. But even Strasser knew that something would have to be done to reduce Germany's airship losses.

He found an answer in the so-called height climbers, a generation of dirigibles that could operate above the 11,000- to 13,000-foot ceiling of almost all British fighter planes then being used in home defense. Heavy sacrifices were made to reduce weight so that the new Zeppelins could achieve higher altitudes: One engine was removed, bombloads reduced by half, fuel capacity reduced and machine guns taken out. In addition, the crew's quarters and comforts were eliminated, the control car made smaller and the hull girders lighter. To afford extra protection, the undersides of the new ships were painted black to reduce reflection from English searchlights.

When the first height climber, designated L 42, made its altitude test flight on March 10, 1917, with Strasser on board, it reached almost 20,000 feet. Subsequent ships were streamlined and lightened even more and achieved even greater heights; the L 53, commissioned in August, climbed to 20,700 feet on its first raid, over the British Midlands, in late September.

The height climbers rendered British defenses powerless. Antiaircraft fire could not reach them, and fighter pilots watched in frustration as they passed far overhead.

But the crews of the height climbers paid a price to operate at such altitudes. Navigation became more difficult than ever, for clouds now tended to be below rather than above the ships, and landmarks were more remote and indistinct. The imperfectly understood upper air currents caused greater errors of drift than before. The high-flying ships became heavily dependent on radio bearings to determine their position; they would transmit signals that could be tracked by German stations. These bearings were unreliable at best and the signals some-

Royal Navy blimps escort a wartime convoy off the English coast in this painting done in 1920. The more than 200 blimps used by the British during World War I were highly successful at seeking out, and occasionally attacking, German submarines.

times revealed the Zeppelins' positions to the enemy. But it was the oxygen-thin air and freezing temperatures of the substratosphere that created the severest problems, both for the men and their machines.

Lack of oxygen caused a marked fall-off in engine power. Above 12,000 feet, altitude sickness began, and men experienced a ringing in the ears, dizziness and headache; at still-greater heights, pulse rates increased and breathing became rapid. Maintaining the ship higher than 16,000 feet for four hours or more caused severe head pains, nausea and vomiting. Physical effort—pumping fuel by hand, or simply making the rounds of the ship—left crewmen exhausted and gasping for breath. Some had to lie down in their hammocks, others grew so apathetic and inefficient they were a danger to the ship's safety. Still others collapsed at their posts.

At first the crews were issued bottles of compressed oxygen to inhale above 16,000 feet. But the oxygen in this primitive breathing apparatus was often contaminated with oil, glycerine or other impurities and tasted so foul that men who breathed it were nauseous for two days afterward. On one high-altitude raid, the captain of the L 46 became almost totally incapacitated from the effects of glycerine in his oxygen bottle. Strasser, who happened to be on board, raged at the captain: "What's wrong with you? Why are you standing there with your hands in your pockets?" Then he ordered the watch officer to take command. Not until the ship was down again after its mission did its captain regain full consciousness.

Bitter cold also took its toll. A crew might take off from Germany in a summer afternoon temperature of 86° F. on the ground and that night be flying 20,000 feet over England at 22° F. below zero. There was no heating system on the Zeppelins; the only protection the men had was the clothing they wore—thick woolen underwear, leather flight suits over blue naval uniforms, fur overcoats on top of that. They donned leather helmets and gloves lined with sheep's wool, big felt overshoes, scarves and sometimes sheets of newspaper worn between layers of clothes for extra insulation. And for all of this, they still suffered frostbite and stiffening of the joints.

The low temperatures caused technical breakdowns in the airships as well. Oil lines snapped, oil congealed, radiators froze solid or boiled dry, celluloid windows cracked, and rudder and elevator control cables slackened and jumped their pulleys. Sometimes even the liquid magnetic compass would freeze, a malfunction that led to the demise of at least one high-climber, the L 48.

Commanded on its first bombing raid by Lieutenant Commander Franz Georg Eichler, and with Strasser's deputy, Commander Viktor Schütze, on board, the L 48 dropped its bombs near Harwich shortly before dawn on June 17, 1917. Eichler then turned for home. Believing that he was flying east, away from England and out of danger, he brought the ship down to 13,000 feet. But the compass had frozen and was giving a faulty reading. The L 48 actually was flying north along the

English coast—at an altitude well within range of the British aircraft that soon closed in on it.

Machinist's Mate Heinrich Ellerkamm, bundled into his fur overcoat and huge felt overshoes, was preparing to check a fuel tank above the engine car when he heard in the distance the faint rattle of machine-gun fire. He stepped onto the lateral gangway inside the hull; then he heard another volley. Looking to the rear of the ship, Ellerkamm watched in horror as incendiary bullets tore into the after gas cells. Tiny blue flames flickered among the gasbags, and almost immediately there was a dull *woof* as the first gas cell exploded. More explosions followed as the other gas cells caught fire; flames ignited the collar of Ellerkamm's fur coat and he tried to beat them out with his hands; above him, the whole 600-foot interior of the Zeppelin was ablaze.

Lieutenant Otto Mieth, the L 48's watch officer, was in the control car talking to Commander Schütze when fire illuminated the car as no searchlight ever had. Mieth looked up and saw flames burning the fabric from the skeleton of the hull. He stripped off his bulky overcoat, thinking that if the ship fell into the sea he could save himself by swimming to safety. But the seasoned Schütze knew better. He glanced once at the flames, turned to Mieth and said: "It's all over."

No one else spoke a word, and the only sound in the car was the crackling roar of the flames overhead. The crewmen stood stolidly at their posts, waiting for the end. Then Mieth, deciding to leap to his death rather than be burned alive, sprang toward a window. As he did so, the Zeppelin's bared hull tipped rearward into a vertical position, upending the control car and hurling its occupants into a corner. Mieth found himself under a pile of his comrades. The L 48 plunged tail first and, as the flames licked at the knot of bodies in the car, Mieth wrapped his arms around his head and hoped that death would come quickly.

Inside the blazing hull, Machinist's Mate Ellerkamm clung desperately to a girder. The sleeve of his coat caught fire and he could feel the searing heat through his overshoes. He was still debating whether or not to jump when the Zeppelin's stern smashed to earth with a prolonged, metallic roar. The superstructure crashed around him. He saw burning fuel from the ruptured tanks flowing toward him like liquid fire. Summoning all his strength he pulled at the mesh of twisted girders that surrounded him and managed to break free. He rolled away from the flaming wreckage until he felt the cool, wet grass of the English meadow. He was alive! Horses were galloping past him, their tails in the air; a wild duck was flying gracefully overhead. And as Ellerkamm gazed up to the early-morning sky through which he had just fallen, the shaken—but virtually uninjured—airshipman saw the British fighter plane whose incendiary bullets had brought down the L 48. The pilot, Lieutenant L. P. Watkins, was circling low to observe his handiwork; he spotted the German survivor, leaned out of his cockpit and waved to him.

Ellerkamm, hoping that others in the 21-man crew might be alive, struggled to his feet and turned back to the burning Zeppelin. He heard

The high-altitude airship L 48 (above) displays the black dope painted on its cotton underside to conceal it from British searchlights during night raids. At right, to confuse enemy bombers, the doors of the airship hangar at Mannheim-Sandhofen are camouflaged as a woodland scene.

Mieth groaning in the control car. The watch officer had suffered burns and both his legs were broken. With the help of British villagers who had rushed to the scene, Ellerkamm pulled Mieth away from the wreckage. Never again during the War would as many as two men survive the crash of a burning Zeppelin.

The L 48 was not the first of the new type of Zeppelins to fall to British guns—nor was England the only place where German airshipmen were in peril. Three days earlier the L 43, with 24 men on board, had been blasted from the skies while on a low-level scouting mission over the German-controlled sector of the North Sea. A month before that, the obsolescent L 22 had gone down in flames with its crew of 21 while on similar duty. Both were victims of a surprise British offensive made possible by the use of new, long-range Curtiss flying boats built in the United States. Based on a somewhat smaller plane, the *America,* designed in 1914 for an attempt to cross the Atlantic that the War had aborted, the flying boats were known as Large Americas.

Henceforth, Zeppelins on scouting operations for the German fleet over the North Sea would be ordered to fly at the same high altitudes as they did on bombing runs over Britain—a minimum of 13,000 feet. But at such altitudes they were almost useless, for they could see neither submarines nor mines, or even correctly identify large ships.

Both as bomber and as strategic scout, the Zeppelin was being replaced by the airplane. By late summer of 1917 large formations of twin-engined Gothas—soon to be joined by four-engined Giants— were raiding the heart of London both at night and in broad daylight. Scarce raw materials such as rubber and aluminum, needed in airship construction, were diverted to the production of planes for an expanding German Air Force; the Navy's airship allotment was limited to 25, and new ships could be built at the rate of only one every two months.

To conserve existing strength, it was decided that raids would be conducted only on extremely dark, cloudy nights—and then only with the greatest caution.

Such a night came on October 19, 1917, and Strasser launched an 11-ship attack that became known in England as the "silent raid." The Zeppelin height climbers flew so high that their engines could not be heard on the ground. Strasser had chosen industrial centers in central England as his targets, but he was to be frustrated once more. As the airships made their landfall they were surprised by a violent north wind that broke up the attack and swept the ships helplessly southward across England at speeds of 45 to 50 miles per hour.

It was hard enough even to recognize a target in these conditions— the commander of one ship thought he had bombed Birmingham and London when in fact he was over Arras, France—but it would prove even harder to get home to Germany. From control cars four miles above southern England, the airshipmen could see the tireless flickering of guns along the trench lines of the Western Front; they realized that the wind was driving them toward that deadly gantlet.

There was little the ships could do to change course in such a wind. Held firmly in the grip of the gale, the L 44 was shot down by French guns with the loss of all 18 hands. The L 49 was forced to land by French fighter planes and its crew was taken prisoner. By coincidence, the L 50 crash-landed in almost the same spot as the L 49, then rose again and drifted away with four men still on board; it was last seen wallowing southward toward the Mediterranean Sea. Lieutenant Commander Hans Kurt Flemming flew his L 55 safely over the Western Front by rising to 24,000 feet (a world altitude for airships that has never been surpassed), but the L 55, almost out of fuel, was wrecked during its forced landing in central Germany. The L 45 succeeded in bombing London when the gale swept it directly across the capital. Trying to return home, however, it was driven so far off course that its captain and crew crash-landed, lost, exhausted and out of fuel, in the Basse-Alpes of southeastern France.

The loss of five Zeppelins was a bitter price to pay for a single, ineffectual raid. The despair of Germany's airshipmen was lifted—at least for a time—by the epic flight of a lone Zeppelin, operating far from the battle routes across the North Sea. The flight had little effect on the course of the War, but it offered a promise for the Zeppelin's peacetime future.

On November 21, 1917, Navy Zeppelin L 59 under Lieutenant Commander Ludwig Bockholt left Jamboli, Bulgaria, the southernmost German airship base on the Eastern Front. Bockholt's mission was to ferry some 14 tons of weapons and medical supplies to the hard-pressed forces of General Paul von Lettow-Vorbeck, who was fighting a desperate rear-guard action against the British in the Makonde Highlands of

German East Africa, now part of Tanzania. The 3,600-mile flight was considered nearly impossible: No airship had ever flown so far, much less under the blistering equatorial sun. No return flight was expected.

The Zeppelin flew via Turkey and Crete to the Mediterranean coast of Egypt. Then it proceeded southward over a landscape such as no airship had ever crossed—a scorching wilderness whose sands reflected the sun's glare so brightly that many of the crew members were stricken with headaches and hallucinations from eye fatigue. Hot-air currents rocked the ship so violently that the elevator man needed all his strength to hold his wheel steady. Even seasoned crewmen became airsick under the violent buffeting.

Commander Bockholt picked his way unerringly across this trackless void, largely by means of celestial navigation. At dusk on November 22, he reached the Nile near its second cataract, above Wadi Halfa. Through the brilliant desert night, the L 59 continued southward toward Khartoum. Ahead lay middle Africa—the barely explored wastes of Kordofan, the swamps of the White Nile, the rain forests of the equatorial highlands and the grass plains of Tanganyika. Any mishap would leave the Zeppelin stranded without hope of rescue in wild and hostile territory controlled by the British, if by anyone at all.

The 22 men of Bockholt's crew were sustained by the knowledge that they were already halfway to their rendezvous with Lettow-Vorbeck's forces. Then in the early hours of November 23, while about 125 miles west of Khartoum, the airshipmen received a radio message from the German Admiralty via the powerful overseas transmitter near Berlin; Lettow-Vorbeck's forces, according to the message, had been overwhelmed by the British. The transmission concluded with an order to the rescue ship: TURN BACK IMMEDIATELY.

Bockholt could not know that the Admiralty's intelligence was faulty, and that Lettow-Vorbeck still held out. With a heavy heart he turned back (and by doing so avoided the aircraft that the British, forewarned, had waiting to intercept him). At 7:40 a.m. on November 25, the L 59 and its 22 adventurers landed safely back at Jamboli. Their 95-hour flight had covered 4,200 miles through the greatest extremes of climate yet experienced by an airship, and they had enough fuel left for another 64 hours. Such endurance, it was noted, would have taken them across the Atlantic and the United States to San Francisco, nonstop.

The L 59's spectacular long-distance performance gave only a temporary lift to disheartened German airshipmen. Less than six weeks later, on January 5, 1918, a series of mysterious explosions destroyed the Naval Airship Division's huge Zeppelin base at Ahlhorn. It was the blackest day thus far in the history of dirigibles. Four hangars were reduced to rubble, five airships destroyed, 10 men killed and 134 injured. After that, although Zeppelins were still being dispatched on occasional raids against England, their day as a military weapon was drawing rapidly to an end.

Peter Strasser still dreamed of dealing a devastating blow with his beloved airships. On August 5, 1918, he set out for England on board the L 70, a Zeppelin of a new and advanced type. Nearly 700 feet long, the L 70 had a gas capacity of 2,195,800 cubic feet, a maximum ceiling of 23,000 feet and a bomb capacity of 8,000 pounds. Seven Maybach high-altitude engines, capable of driving it at 81 miles per hour, made the L 70 the fastest airship yet built.

In company with four older airships, the L 70 steered for the enemy coastline. Three British planes rushed out to intercept the invaders. Cruising at about 17,000 feet—well below his ship's potential—

An unlikely capture at sea

"Prepare to board our prize!" The order, unique in aviation history, was given by Captain Ludwig Bockholt of the airship L 23 on April 23, 1917, to the delight of his crew. Approaching the Norwegian schooner *Royal* near Denmark, the Germans had seen panicky sailors abandoning ship and guessed they were bound for England with embargoed cargo (it turned out to be mining timbers).

When a boarding party from L 23 dropped into a lifeboat, the lightened airship shot upward, taking with it the party's machine gun. Brandishing a signaling pistol, the Germans bluffed the ship's crew into submission and sailed the prize triumphantly to port.

An artist's rendition of the capture of the schooner Royal by airship L 23 minimizes the actual difficulties caused by wind and high seas.

Strasser believed that he was immune to enemy aircraft. But a swift de Havilland D.H.4 two-seater rose to meet him, climbing to 16,400 feet for the attack. Approaching head on from below, the British gunner pumped explosive bullets into the Zeppelin's mammoth hull. Almost at once it burst into flames, sank by its stern and fell. A British airman wrote later that as the blazing mass dropped through the upper cloud layers, the clouds "threw back immense fans of light, making everything about us as bright as day. Slowly the reflected brilliance faded, until only a pinpoint of light, far down in the cloud mass, was left to indicate the course of the falling wreckage." There were no survivors; Strasser's body, recovered by the British, was buried at sea.

The other Zeppelins on the raid scattered and made it safely home, but Germany's once-vaunted naval airship fleet had effectively perished with Strasser. Zeppelins still flew from time to time on naval scouting missions as they had done throughout the War, but there were no more raids on England. By the autumn of 1918 it was clear that Germany was losing and the end was near. On October 28, a mutiny broke out among disaffected sailors of the High Seas Fleet and spread to the Naval Airship Division. The air crews remained loyal to the Kaiser, but the ground crewmen took over the bases, arrested their officers and sent them home. By November 9, two days before the Armistice, the Zeppelins had been deflated and hung up in their hangars.

For the German airships that once had tried to win the War almost singlehandedly, the defeat was all but total. With the possible exception of the U-boat service, no arm of the German Navy had suffered such heavy percentage losses. More than 40 per cent of the Navy's airship crewmen had been killed and 53 of its 73 airships destroyed by enemy action or by accidents. The Army had suffered lighter casualties but had lost 26 of its 50 ships.

In sum, the actual damages inflicted on the enemy were relatively slight. During 51 airship raids on England, for example, 557 Britons were killed and 1,358 injured. Property damage from the dropping of 196 tons of bombs amounted to £1.5 million—a mere pinprick in the British hide. Indirectly, the raids were more effective: They added to the war weariness of the British people, tied up troops and planes that might have been used on the battlefield and, perhaps most important, they satisfied a deeply felt need of the German people to carry the War to the enemy's homeland in retaliation for Britain's rigorous blockade of the fatherland.

In the tumultuous months following the Armistice, the airship bases were looted and the supplies and equipment sold on the black market. On June 21, 1919, German crews of the High Seas Fleet scuttled their impounded ships at Scapa Flow. Two days later, the Zeppelin crews followed suit, destroying seven of Germany's remaining Navy airships by letting them fall heavily to their hangar floors. It was an act of defiance by proud men who, though defeated, wanted to keep Count von Zeppelin's uniquely German creations out of alien hands.

3
Probing new horizons of distance flight

Perched informally atop a water tank in the control car of His Majesty's Airship R 34, Brigadier General Edward Maitland watched the Long Island landscape rolling gently by beneath him. As the British Air Ministry's Director of Airships, Maitland had ample cause for contentment, for the R 34 was about to complete the first east-to-west transatlantic flight in history. "As we skim over this American countryside," he wrote in his personal logbook, "I confess to a delightful glow of satisfaction at gazing on American soil for the first time—from above. It brings home to me more than anything else could ever do, what a small place this world really is, what an astonishing part these great Airship Liners will play in linking together the remotest places of the earth; and what interesting years lie immediately ahead!"

It was the morning of July 6, 1919, and with the flight of the R 34, a new era of airship development and exploration was beginning. The hydrogen-filled rigid airship had failed, in the end, as a weapon of war. But during the first years of peace it was still the only kind of aircraft capable of transoceanic, intercontinental passenger flight, or of the exploration by air of vast regions of the globe that were still uncharted. At this moment only Great Britain was prepared to exploit these opportunities. Germany had been vanquished, its surviving war dirigibles allocated as reparations to the victorious Allies, and most of its airship installations dismantled or destroyed. The Zeppelin Company, like much of Germany's industry, faced a fight for mere economic survival.

The British had confined their wartime lighter-than-air operations mostly to nonrigid airships—for which they had coined the word "blimp," supposedly from the plopping sound made by the envelope whenever someone flicked a finger on it to test the pressure of the gas inside. They had deployed the sturdy little blimps on antisubmarine patrols, reconnaisance flights and convoy-escort duty.

Britain had far less success with the eight rigids it flew during the War. But in 1916 the German Zeppelin L 33 had been forced down on English soil; though it was badly damaged, the British were able to copy from it in building their own postwar ships, and with the launching of the

Climbing into the predawn darkness, the British airship R 34 takes off from Scotland on the 2nd of July, 1919, to attempt the first round-trip aerial crossing of the Atlantic Ocean. The R 34's voyage signaled the beginning of an era of long-distance airship travel.

R (for rigid) 33 and the R 34 in March 1919, Britain possessed two of the best airships in the world. Measuring 643 feet long and with a gas capacity of just under two million cubic feet, the British rigids were each fitted with five engines that could drive them up to 55 miles per hour.

Just weeks after its maiden flight, the R 34 was ordered to prepare for an unprecedented Atlantic crossing. The official reason for the trip was to display the new ship at the May meeting of the Aero Club of America. But the real purpose was to demonstrate the feasibility of flying passenger airships over long-distance routes.

The R 34, damaged during a test flight, did not get under way in time to make the Aero Club appearance. Meanwhile, the Atlantic was crossed twice by airplane in the spring of 1919—first by a United States Navy flying boat that made it from Newfoundland to Portugal (with a refueling stop in the Azores), and then by former Royal Air Force fliers John Alcock and Arthur Whitten Brown, who flew nonstop from Newfoundland to Ireland in a converted Vickers Vimy bomber. Still, no airplane of the day had enough endurance to buck the head winds of an east-to-west Atlantic flight. Nor had any airplane attempted a round trip. The R 34 could still be a pioneer.

At 1:42 a.m. on July 2, 1919, the R 34 lifted off from its base at East Fortune in Scotland with 30 men on its crew and passenger list. The airship's captain was Major George Herbert Scott, one of Britain's most experienced dirigible pilots. The senior officer on board, General Maitland, was the driving force behind Britain's airship program. A popular 39-year-old officer, Maitland had devoted his career to innovative flight of all kinds. He had built one of Britain's first military airplanes, had once made a 1,100-mile free balloon flight from London to Russia, and in a wartime demonstration had been the first man to parachute out of an airship. He became such an advocate of parachutes, in fact, that with few exceptions he climaxed every airship flight he made by enthusiastically chuting to earth ahead of his ship.

Above all, Maitland was a believer in the future of rigid dirigibles, and as the R 34 groped its way westward at 1,500 feet through the dense clouds and inky blackness of a windy Highland night, he shared in the intense excitement on board. The R 34 was a trailblazer, and all hands knew it. "What more wonderful or more delightful adventure could anyone be called upon to undertake?" Maitland had written in his logbook as he stood in the control car just before takeoff. At 5:25 a.m., two hours after the sun had risen behind the ship, the R 34 passed the last island off the north Irish coast. The great crossing had begun.

Not until the R 34 had left the land well behind was it discovered that there was an unauthorized passenger on board. At the last minute, Aircraftsman Second Class William W. Ballantyne had been dropped from the crew to save weight, but he was so eager to make the journey that he had stowed away in the hull, emerging after the ship had been aloft for 12 hours. If the R 34 had still been over land, Ballantyne would

In a large double hangar at East Fortune, Scotland, airships R 34 (left) and R 29 are berthed prior to the R 34's flight to the United States in 1919. The smaller R 29 had served with distinction on antisubmarine patrols late in World War I.

have been ordered overboard by parachute, but now there was no alternative but to take him on to America.

Major Scott had three chief concerns as he guided his ship across the ocean—conserving gas and ballast, economizing on fuel and navigating a straight course. To avoid the expansion and subsequent loss of gas through superheating in the sun, he flew inside clouds and fog whenever possible. To save fuel he frequently used only two to four of the ship's five engines. So precisely did Scott handle his craft that when the navigator wanted to take a sun shot with his sextant from the gun platform at the top of the hull, Scott took the ship up until the navigator's head was just clear, while the rest of his body and the whole of the giant dirigible remained buried inside the clouds.

When the second dawn broke, the R 34 was well over halfway from Ireland to Newfoundland; Scott calculated that he could make the remaining 750 nautical miles to Cape Race, Newfoundland, in about 24 hours. Shortly after noon the clouds cleared and the men of the R 34 got their first panoramic view of the Atlantic—a vast expanse of blue water punctuated by whitecapped waves. For a time, the ship surged forward at nearly 40 knots, but that evening the wind backed and blew up to a gale. In thick fog and bitter cold the R 34 had to fight its way forward while rain, driven by savage gusts, beat such a thunderous tattoo on the hull that crewmen had to shout to be heard. The sea beneath them was lashed white by the wind, but the airship held a steady course.

By dawn of July 4—the third day out—the skies had cleared and the crew stared down at a dazzling iceberg, their first sign of having crossed to a strange quarter of the globe. Fog engulfed them again, but shortly after noon Scott caught sight of land. "This is quite the most thrilling moment of our voyage," General Maitland wrote. "Whether or not we now succeed in getting through to New York, we have at any rate successfully accomplished the first stage of our adventure, and are the first to bridge the gulf from East to West by way of the air."

At 1:30 p.m. the R 34 crossed the coast of Newfoundland and by evening it was passing Nova Scotia. New York was still some 800 miles away and Scott had signaled to his landing party, already in place at Mineola, Long Island, that he expected to arrive there early on Sunday morning, July 6. But fuel had now run dangerously low—a little more than 2,000 gallons remained at the latest check—and when the ship ran into strong head winds that night the chance of reaching New York without having to make an intermediate refueling stop seemed slim. "Too depressing!" noted Maitland.

All morning on Saturday, July 5—the fourth day of the voyage—the R 34 butted against the ceaseless wind. To economize on fuel, Scott ran the ship on only three engines, and to avoid the worst of the winds he flew at 800 feet—as low as he dared go. Reluctantly, he radioed for United States Navy destroyers to stand by off Cape Cod so the airship could be refueled at sea or taken in tow if the need arose. He also advised that he might have to refuel at the Naval Air Station at Chatham, Massachusetts, or at Montauk, on the eastern tip of Long Island.

The situation grew more serious that afternoon when a major storm moved across the ship's path. In the control car, the first warning came when the storm's electrical activity caused the compass card to spin like a top. Then a squall hit the ship, forcing it up and down at alarming angles. The engines, unable to function properly at such steep inclines, cut out and then cut in again with a frightening spurt of naked flame from the exhaust pipes. The girders creaked like the timbers of an old sailing ship and the chief engineer was nearly thrown out of the hull through a hatch; he saved himself by hooking a foot around a girder. Later, violent updrafts and downdrafts, caused by sudden variations in sea temperature, threw the ship up 400 feet, then dropped it 500, while the tail flexed alarmingly with the strain. That night the crew wore parachutes and kept life belts close at hand.

Before dawn on Sunday, Scott made a decision. He radioed the Navy: "Will land Montauk." Shortly after 4 a.m. the airshipmen caught their first sight of the distinctive United States coastline at Cape Cod.

In the last hours of its voyage, fortune began to favor the R 34. A following wind had increased the ship's speed during the night so that by breakfast time Long Island was in sight on the far horizon. A foraging party armed with cooking pots and empty jars had collected every drop of fuel from the ship's 81 tanks, and concentrated it in the gravity tanks immediately above the engines. At 7:20 a.m. the airship appeared over Montauk, but instead of landing, Scott decided to try to make the last 90 miles to Mineola, his original goal.

There had never been a rigid airship in America before, and no one had ever seen anything like the R 34, floating majestically in from the Old World with the morning sun. A host of spectators converged on Mineola and 500 military policemen were detailed to control them. On hand to help land the craft were more than 1,000 men from the United States Navy Air Service. What was missing, however, was an officer with any experience at landing a giant rigid airship, for the commander of the R 34's own advance landing party had rushed off to Boston when it was thought the ship would make a fueling stop in Massachusetts. The only solution was for one of the R 34's officers to parachute from the ship and take over arrangements on the ground. Major J. E. M. Pritchard volunteered, and became the first man ever to arrive in America by air. Landing heavily, he was instantly surrounded by reporters.

"Can you tell us what your first impressions of America are, sir?" asked one of them.

"Hard," replied Pritchard. Then he rode off on a motorbike to the spot where the R 34 was maneuvering toward a gentler descent.

When the ship came down at 9:54 a.m., it had spent 108 hours and 12 minutes in the air—a new record—and thanks to the crew's conservation efforts, had enough fuel left for two more hours at full throttle. "We couldn't have cut it much finer," concluded Maitland in his log.

The 31 officers and crew were feted as pioneers and heroes. They had taken almost as long as a steamship to cross the Atlantic, and nearly seven times longer than Alcock and Brown had needed in their Vickers Vimy, flying eastward, a few weeks earlier. Nonetheless, they had shown the way—or so it seemed—to the future of transatlantic travel. They had flown in relative comfort, and their aircraft had landed at their announced destination intact. Alcock and Brown may have traveled faster, but they had flown upside down at one point, their heads almost touching the water, and had landed nose down in an Irish bog.

After the crew had enjoyed three days of heady celebration in New York City, the R 34 took off from Mineola for the return flight. With the wind on its tail—pushing its ground speed at times up to 90 miles per hour—the airship completed the crossing in just over three days. The British press hailed the achievement. Ironically, however, neither the British public nor the government responded to the airship's return with anything like the excitement it had spawned in the United States.

Britain's economy, in fact, was going through a difficult period of postwar adjustment and its airship program was soon stifled by austerity and neglect. Finally the budget-minded government ordered the closing of the airship service on August 1, 1921. By then the R 34 had already been dismantled, after being severely damaged on the ground by heavy winds, and the R 33, which had made several successful flights over the British Isles, was retired. The only rigid airship in which the British continued an active interest was the R 38—which was being built for sale to the United States Navy.

Alone among the leading air-minded nations, the United States still saw a military use for rigid airships as strategic scouts for the fleet, particularly in the Pacific, where distances were vast and American outposts widely scattered. Moreover, the Americans possessed an element that promised to make their airships far safer to operate than any that had come before. The substance was helium, a rare inert gas first isolated in 1895 and found virtually nowhere in the world except in Texas and parts of Kansas. Helium weighed twice as much as hydrogen, and under comparable conditions had only 92.6 per cent as much lifting capacity. It also was many times more expensive. Available at the time only through a single, not very efficient plant in Fort Worth, it cost some $120 per 1,000 cubic feet, compared with two or three dollars for a like amount of hydrogen. However, unlike hydrogen, helium was nonflammable; its use would almost eliminate the risk of fire aloft.

In 1919 the United States Congress had appropriated funds for a large Navy airship base and the acquisition of two large rigid airships. One of the ships, the ZR 1, was to be built in the United States; the other was the British-built R 38, which the Americans intended to designate ZR 2. (All of the Navy's lighter-than-air craft were given a Z designation—unofficially for Zeppelin-type; the R stood for rigid.)

The 2,724,000-cubic-foot R 38 was the biggest airship of its day. Conceived in 1918 as a high-altitude, high-performance North Sea

The making of a leakproof cell

These photographs of British women at work in the Short Brothers' factory in 1919 trace the manufacture of one of an airship's crucial parts: its gas cells. The linen cells were lined with layers of membrane, obtained from the intestines of cattle and called goldbeater's skin because it was used by artisans to contain gold as they hammered it into gold leaf.

Strong and lightweight, goldbeater's skin was the most gastight of any flexible material, and it would neither rip nor give off dangerous sparks when rubbed. It was also very expensive. One steer yielded a membrane no more than 10 by 40 inches in size, and each gas cell required some 50,000 such skins. The cost of a single cell was £2,000—and each airship had from 15 to 20 cells.

Women scrape goldbeater's skins clean, moistening each frequently in a brine solution.

In the cavernous factory, the women at tables stick goldbeater's skins together (right) and glue them to a linen panel (left).

Once all the panels have been stitched together, two dozen workers roll up the finished cell to await testing.

Inside a partially inflated cell, kneeling workers patch holes while inspectors in soft footwear scrutinize the sides for leaks.

patrol ship and already under construction when the Americans put in their bid in 1919, it was intended to outperform the best German Zeppelin ever built. But few British or American airshipmen were aware that a light-framed height climber could be safely maneuvered only at high altitudes, where the air was thin and the aerodynamic stresses less than at lower levels. During the R 38's preliminary trials whole girders had buckled from the strain of sharp turns at low altitudes. But this caused no general alarm. Indeed, the flight tests were curtailed—partly for economy's sake on the part of the British, partly out of impatience on the part of the Americans, who were anxious to fly their new ship home before the arrival of uncertain fall weather.

On August 24, 1921, while the R 38 was undergoing a final test flight with a mixed British and American crew, the British captain put it through a series of violent maneuvers. At a speed of more than 60 miles per hour and an altitude of only 2,500 feet, the helmsman moved the rudder repeatedly hard to port, to starboard, then back again. It was too much. The ship broke in two just behind the rear-engine gondolas.

People on the ground saw the R 38 crumple and heard an immense explosion as the gas cells—still filled with hydrogen—blew up, shattering the windows of houses for miles around. The forward half of the ship plunged in flames into the Humber River, and only one survivor was pulled from the wreckage. The rear half came down more slowly, landing on a sandbar; five men, including the sole survivor of the American contingent on board, were rescued. Sixteen Americans and 28 Britons, including the great airship advocate Edward Maitland, died in the crash.

The R 38 disaster did little to dampen American enthusiasm. At the Naval Aircraft Factory in Philadelphia, work was started on the ZR 1, and in June 1922 the United States Navy signed a contract with the Zeppelin Company for construction in Germany of a replacement for the ill-fated R 38. In September of the following year, the ZR 1—the first rigid airship to be inflated with helium—made its maiden flight from the two-year-old airship base at Lakehurst, New Jersey. The 680-foot craft had been christened U.S.S. *Shenandoah,* an Indian name that is popularly translated as "Daughter of the Stars."

The Navy had ambitious plans for its new ship: It was decided that in the spring of 1924 the *Shenandoah* would make an exploratory flight to the North Pole, which had been reached only once before, by land, in 1909. Plans were made to erect a series of mooring masts—a British innovation—to which an airship could be tethered by means of a nose fitting, thus permitting it to swing freely in the wind. The masts would be placed at intervals across America, and on a ship that would be stationed in the Arctic.

The crew of the *Shenandoah,* preparing for their great adventure, expected to be first to the Pole by air, and their expectation seemed reasonable enough. Airplanes of the day lacked the range for polar flights, and only three other rigid airships were flying anywhere in the world—two in France and one in Italy.

Rescue craft stand by helplessly in this depiction by an Italian artist of the crash of the R 38 into England's Humber River in 1921. In reality the R 38 had broken in half in a thick fog, and the stern section had landed safely with four of the airship's five survivors on board.

Of these, only the French *Dixmude,* a war-reparations Zeppelin, was capable of anything more ambitious than a short-range training flight. Commanded by an outstanding French Navy airshipman, Lieutenant Jean du Plessis de Grenedan, the *Dixmude* had performed a number of impressive feats, including a long flight to the Sahara that extended the world record for endurance in the air to 118 hours 41 minutes. Then, in the early hours of December 21, 1923, while returning to France from a long-distance flight over Algeria and Tunisia, the *Dixmude* caught fire and exploded in a violent thunderstorm over the Mediterranean. A few shattered bits of wreckage and two identifiable corpses—one of them du Plessis—were all that was found of the giant air cruiser and its 50 men. It was the worst air disaster to date, and it marked the end of France's rigid-airship program.

American airshipmen were little bothered by news of the *Dixmude's* loss, but the *Shenandoah's* Arctic flight had to be postponed when it was damaged after being blown away from its mast in a gale. When the *Shenandoah* next took to the air in May 1924 it was under the command of a new skipper, Lieutenant Commander Zachary Lansdowne.

At the age of 35, Lansdowne was one of a handful of American officers with measurable airship experience. He had been on board the British R 34 as an observer during its flight from England to the United States in 1919 and later, in a Navy blimp, had successfully tested the feasibility of helium as a successor to hydrogen. He was also preparing a pioneering manual on the operation of large rigid airships. In it, Lansdowne included such practical recommendations as two-piece flight suits for air crews instead of the bulky one-piece design, uncoded radio transmissions during the tricky stages of landing and mooring, and a less exhausting watch schedule of four hours on, eight off instead of the previous four on, four off. He also warned against flying in or near thunderstorms, with their wrenching updrafts and downdrafts, regardless of whether the airship was filled with hydrogen or helium.

As a warm-up for the Arctic venture, Lansdowne was charged with executing a major cross-country demonstration flight: From Lakehurst, the *Shenandoah* was to fly across the United States to California, then north to Washington State and back across the country to Lakehurst.

The flight got under way on October 7, 1924, and it enchanted Americans as fully as the flights of Count von Zeppelin's prewar airships had captivated the German public. And when the *Shenandoah* returned triumphantly to its home base on October 25—after a round trip of 235 hours and 1 minute in the air, with several stops along the way— it was moored alongside the new ZR 3, the replacement ship that had flown in from Germany only 10 days earlier.

Unfortunately, there was only enough of the scarce and expensive helium for one big airship, and while the *Shenandoah's* transcontinental flight was hailed on both sides of the Atlantic as the forerunner of a commercial passenger airship service, the big airship's glory was soon cut short. The helium from the *Shenandoah* was pumped into the ZR 3, now named the U.S.S. *Los Angeles,* and until the summer of 1925 the *Shenandoah* was laid up in the huge hangar at Lakehurst. By the time it took to the air again the costly—and risky—Arctic flight plan had been scrapped; instead of making history at the North Pole, the ship would make routine demonstration flights in the American Midwest.

On September 2, 1925, the *Shenandoah* cast off from Lakehurst with 43 men on board, bound for St. Louis, Minneapolis and Detroit. Very early the next day it was over Ohio and heading west into a region notorious for its violent storms. At about 3 a.m., just north of the small town of Ava, vivid flashes of lightning alerted the watch to gathering thunderstorms in the north and east. An ominous black cloud now blocked the path westward, but the skies to the south and southwest were still clear; Lansdowne ordered the *Shenandoah's* course changed slightly to the south, though the ship was now confronted with gale-force winds that reduced its ground speed almost to zero. The *Shenandoah* struggled to stay on course, but Lansdowne did not feel in any immediate danger and decided against diverting due south, where the weather remained clear. At about the same time, a huge streaky cloud was forming above and to the right of the ship—"as though two storms had got together," in the words of an eyewitness on the ground.

Suddenly the elevator man exclaimed: "The ship is rising a meter a second, Captain!" Lansdowne ordered him to check the ascent. The elevator man forced his wheel hard over until the ship's bow was pointing down at an angle of 18 degrees, but it was no use. "I can't hold her down," he reported. Meanwhile, Lansdowne at last had ordered the helmsman to turn south toward clear weather.

The ship was driven rapidly skyward by irresistible currents of warm air. At 3,000 feet, pitching and reeling, it leveled off for a moment. Then it rose even faster, at a breathtaking 1,000 feet per minute.

By now captain and crew knew they were helpless captives in the ferocious storm. Finally, at about 6,200 feet, the *Shenandoah's* ascent was checked. Then the ship began to fall. So much gas had been valved to check the climb that the craft dropped at 1,500 feet per minute— even faster than it had risen. More than 4,000 pounds of water ballast was let go to slow the descent, and the crew stood by to jettison fuel tanks and thus lighten the ship still further. But at 3,000 feet the fall was checked with a jolt by another swiftly rising current of air. The airship began to spin wildly, its hull writhing from the strain.

Once more the *Shenandoah* began to rise. The nose went up and up until it was pointing sharply toward the sky. At the same time turbulent winds hammered at the hull, forcing the nose to port and the tail to starboard, wringing the 680-foot-long Daughter of the Stars like a wet rag. At last, with a tremendous roaring of rent metal, the airship broke in two.

The men stationed in the control car heard the awful sound and felt the car shudder as it began to tear loose from the hull. "Anyone who wants to leave the car may do so," Lansdowne said quietly. Two of the men scrambled up the ladder into the forward hull section. The ones

Disappearing into the morning mist, the LZ 126 departs Friedrichshafen in 1924 for its new home in Lakehurst, New Jersey, where it will be renamed the U.S.S. Los Angeles. The ship completed its 5,000-mile westward passage in 81 hours—an average speed of about 62 miles per hour.

Lifted by a breeze that swept under its tail, the Los Angeles stands on end for a precarious moment above the 160-foot mooring mast at Lakehurst in August 1927. Inside, 25 crewmen hung on as tools, spare parts and other loose articles ripped through the ship's outer cover. Then the airship gently returned to a normal position, on the other side of its pivotal mast.

who remained, including Lansdowne, stood frozen to their duty posts.

For a brief time the two sections of the ship were held together by the control cables that ran through the keel from the control car to the rudder and elevators. But the weight of the car soon wrenched the cables loose, and the car and its eight occupants fell like a stone. Six more crewmen—two in the radio car and four in the forward-engine gondolas—plunged to the ground seconds later. The ship's still-buoyant bow section, with seven men inside, broke away and floated up to a height of 10,000 feet. The stern section split in two, and one part, the 425-foot-long tail with 14 men on board, glided to earth and landed heavily but safely. The other part, carrying four men, floated down even more gently, its fall cushioned by a stand of trees. The seven men in the ballooning 200-foot bow section, led by the 33-year-old navigator Lieutenant Commander Charles E. Rosendahl, finally brought themselves to the ground by valving gas. They landed safely at 6:45 a.m.—nearly an hour after Lansdowne and those with him in the control car had plunged to their death. In all, 29 of the 43 men who had set out on the *Shenandoah* survived the disaster, mainly because the ship's gasbags had been filled with helium rather than with highly explosive hydrogen.

The catastrophe had a morbid aftermath. The few segments of the *Shenandoah* had all fallen in remote parts of Ohio. All through the day that followed, swarms of curiosity seekers looted the various parts of wreckage, picking them almost clean. Some of the gas cells wound up in the hands of a tailor in Marietta, who turned them into raincoats that he advertised for sale as Shenandoah Slickers.

The *Shenandoah* was gone, but its original mission—to fly over the North Pole—was not forgotten. Norwegian explorer Roald Amundsen, who in 1911 had been the first man to reach the South Pole, had failed in an attempt to reach the North Pole by airplane. In 1926 he tried again—this time in an Italian-built semirigid dirigible that was smaller, lighter and far less costly than ships of the *Shenandoah* class.

Amundsen, now 53, bought his airship from the Italian government with funds provided by a wealthy American, Lincoln Ellsworth, who had accompanied Amundsen on his unsuccessful polar airplane flight the previous year. Not quite 350 feet long and fitted with three Maybach engines that gave it a top speed of 70 miles per hour, the craft had an anticipated cruising range of some 3,500 miles. The patriotic Norwegian named the airship *Norge,* and placed it under the command of its Italian designer, Umberto Nobile, a courageous and ambitious airshipman with a strong patriotic streak of his own.

On April 10, 1926, three days before Amundsen and Ellsworth arrived at the expedition's starting point at King's Bay, on the Arctic island of Spitsbergen, the *Norge* took off from Rome on the first leg of its long journey. Nobile chose a zigzag course via the few airship bases then existing in Europe, stopping in England, Norway and Russia, where his hosts quartered him in what had been the Imperial Palace and fitted him

The death agony of the Shenandoah, which was wrenched beyond its endurance by a violent squall on September 3, 1925, is dramatized in this oil painting.

Souvenir hunters and the plain curious flock to the field in eastern Ohio where the tail section of the Shenandoah had come down. The bow had landed 12 miles away.

with warm boots made from swatches of the deposed Czar's carpets.

Nobile reached King's Bay on May 7. There he found that the *Norge* had been preceded by an unexpected and uninvited group of rivals, Americans commanded by Navy Lieutenant Richard E. Byrd. Byrd had with him a powerful Fokker ski plane with which he intended to make the first polar flight ahead of the Amundsen party. Two days later, while the *Norge* was still being serviced in its roofless hangar, Byrd roared across the ice and took off. Fifteen and a half hours later he returned to report that he had reached the North Pole. (Some people doubted Byrd's claim then, and some still do, on the ground that his craft lacked the range to make the round trip. But the claim is widely and officially accepted.) The *Norge's* only hope for glory now seemed to lie in going beyond the Pole, across the entire Arctic region to North America.

On the morning of May 11, 1926, Nobile cast off and turned north. The Pole lay 770 miles away. From that first goal the *Norge's* route lay straight across more than 1,000 miles of unknown Arctic territory to Point Barrow, on the northern coast of Alaska; from there the airship would follow the coast south to its final destination at Nome, on the Bering Sea. The bitter Arctic weather, the difficulties of navigation over uncharted wastes in the region of the Magnetic Pole, and the slim chance of rescue if things went wrong all combined to make this the most hazardous course an airship had ever attempted. Moreover, the

Norge's safety margin was slim. It could barely lift all that was needed for the flight, and it carried no ballast. Its fuel supply was severely limited; if slowed by fog or strong head winds, it would not have enough fuel to reach Alaska. Despite the hazards, the 16 crewmen—eight Norwegians, six Italians, one American and one Swede, crowded into the engine gondolas and the tiny control car—were filled with optimism.

By noon the *Norge* was droning steadily at 1,350 feet over the frozen ocean, making 50 miles per hour and more on a wind that howled about the ship like a factory whistle. It was the season of constant daylight but the air inside the control car was freezing cold in spite of the sun; the men grew even colder as clouds covered the sky and the airship was beset by snow, fog and ice. The metal outer parts of the ship became caked with ice half an inch thick and ice began to form even inside the control car.

Nobile took the ship up to 3,000 feet, where it was above the fog, and pushed on. Then he began his descent toward the roof of the world, and at 1:30 a.m. on May 12, 1926, at a height of 600 feet, the *Norge* slowly flew over the North Pole. Amundsen commemorated the moment by throwing out a handkerchief-sized Norwegian flag, and Ellsworth dropped a Stars and Stripes of the same modest proportions. Then Nobile, with more pride than tact, hurled out an enormous banner and noted grandly in the ship's log: "Planted the Italian flag at the Pole." It was an act that Amundsen never forgave.

The elation of reaching the Pole soon eroded as the crew realized they now faced by far the longest leg of the journey. The working crewmen numbered only 12, not enough to give them proper rest between stints of duty, and even when they were off duty it was difficult to find a place to sleep. The control car was cold, crowded and squalid. Dozens of Thermos bottles were scattered carelessly across its deck. "In the midst of all this mess," Nobile recorded in his diary, "there stuck out picturesquely Amundsen's enormous feet, with his grass-stuffed shoes." The crew of the *Norge* grew tired. Nobile found one helmsman steering across the featureless waste with his eyes closed; another, hallucinating from extreme exhaustion, insisted that he had seen a squadron of cavalry galloping across the snow.

Amundsen had spent most of the flight staring down at the white wilderness in the hope of discovering unknown land to claim for his native Norway. It was a vain effort. Early on the morning of May 13 the navigator cried: "Land ahead to starboard." It was Alaska, and an hour later the *Norge* made its landfall near Point Barrow. The explorers had completed the first crossing of the Arctic from one edge to the other; they had seen nothing but frozen water all the way.

The expedition had regained the inhabited world, but the men were not yet out of danger. For nearly 24 hours, in a state of utter exhaustion, they groped their way south toward Nome, tossed between Alaska and Siberia by violent crosswinds, flying blind through fog. Despairing at last of reaching Nome in one piece, Nobile decided to bring the *Norge* down near the tiny settlement of Teller, and at 7:30 a.m. on March 14,

Norwegian and Italian ground crewmen walk the Norge into its unique roofless hangar at King's Bay, Spitsbergen, before its polar flight.

watched by a group of startled Eskimos, he made a remarkable unassisted landing on the open ice. There the airship was deflated and dismantled for transportation by sea back to Europe.

The *Norge* had crossed a third of the world, from the Mediterranean to the Pacific via the North Pole, flying a total of 7,800 miles in 171 hours. Its 3,180-mile Arctic crossing had taken 70 hours 40 minutes at an average speed of 45 miles per hour.

It was a supreme achievement, but one that soon provoked bitter dissension. As leader of the expedition, Amundsen claimed credit for the flight. But Nobile, as commander of the airship, got all the recognition. Before leaving America he was widely interviewed by the press, and was received at the White House by President Calvin Coolidge. Italian dictator Benito Mussolini recognized the flight as an exploit that would enhance the prestige of his new Fascist state, and Nobile was given a tumultuous reception when he returned to Rome. The 41-year-old engineer had dazzled the world with one of history's great flights.

Amundsen, galled by the attention paid to Nobile, reacted bitterly. In an autobiography, *My Life As An Explorer,* published in 1927, he devoted 95 pages to attacking the Italian as the "hired skipper of a Norwegian ship owned by an American and myself" who was seeking to "usurp honors that do not belong to him." But Nobile's success had made him enemies far more dangerous than the old Norwegian explorer. Chief among them was Italo Balbo, one of the founding fathers of Italian Fascism and Mussolini's mercurial, talented and ambitious Undersecretary for Air. Balbo did not like airships and he liked Nobile even less; he was soon plotting to demote them both. Believing that Italy's future in the air lay with the airplane (and with himself), Balbo planned to fly huge squadrons of military aircraft on spectacular long-distance formation flights. He scrapped plans for building a big new Italian airship and poisoned Mussolini's mind against Nobile.

As ingenuous as he was sometimes tactless, Nobile was oblivious to his imminent fall from official favor. He pursued his latest plans, which he had hatched barely three days after the completion of the *Norge* flight. On that voyage, Nobile had explored some 50,000 square miles of the unknown Arctic; he now proposed a long series of flights to cover the rest—an estimated 1.5 million square miles—in a second airship, this time named the *Italia.* Though always optimistic, Nobile did not minimize the risks of his undertaking. "We have absolute confidence in the preparation of the expedition," he said during a speech in Milan—whose city government would raise the funds for the expedition through private subscription. "All that could be foreseen has been foreseen—even the possibility of failure or catastrophe. We are quite aware that our venture is difficult and dangerous—even more so than that of 1926—but it is this very difficulty and danger that attracts us. Had it been safe and easy, other people would already have preceded us."

In April of 1928 the *Italia* left Milan and, after a delay in Germany for repairs, reached King's Bay on May 6. The expedition's support vessel,

Colonel Umberto Nobile, the designer and captain of the Norge, takes a last look at Spitsbergen as his ship sets out for the North Pole in 1926. Deeply patriotic, Nobile saw the expedition as a triumph for Italy.

Bundled against the Arctic cold, Norwegian explorer Roald Amundsen occupies his comfortable chair in the Norge's control car. As the expedition's leader, Amundsen regarded Nobile as only a hired pilot.

an aged hulk named *Città di Milano* and captained by a dedicated Fascist named Giuseppe Romagna Manoja, was already there.

After one false start—and a 69-hour exploratory flight that was cut short by bad weather—the explorers set out at 4:28 a.m. on May 23, 1928. The *Italia* bore off to the north for a return to the Pole along a new route, via unexplored territory to the north of Greenland. The airship crossed Spitsbergen and north Greenland, then headed for the Pole in bright sunshine, helped by a strong tail wind. After 20 hours, at 12:20 a.m., the *Italia* reached the Pole and circled, dropping a new Italian flag, the coat of arms of the sponsoring city of Milan, a little medal of the Virgin of Fire and finally a large oak cross provided by Pope Pius XI. Inside the control cabin, the gramophone played ''The Bells of St. Giusto,'' followed by ''Giovinezza,'' the Fascist battle hymn. It was a time of intense emotion for the 16 men on board.

Now Nobile faced a difficult decision. Depending on prevailing winds, he had intended either to circle back over the Arctic island of Severnaya Zemyla, just north of the Siberian land mass, or to continue across the Arctic to northern Canada, staying aloft a week if necessary. Neither option looked particularly good to him. Heavy weather lay ahead, and the friendly wind that had helped him reach the Pole would be dead against him if he turned back. Nobile was half-inclined to risk the run to Canada, but his Swedish meteorologist, Finn Malmgren, predicted that the strong southerly wind would soon give way to a lighter north-westerly. Their best chance, he said, was to return to King's Bay. After two hours at the Pole, Nobile agreed and set course for Spitsbergen.

Malmgren's weather forecast proved faulty, and for 24 hours the *Italia* struggled through fog and snow flurries, making a ground speed of barely 25 miles per hour against rising head winds. Ice formed a thick layer all over the ship's exterior, and the propellers hurled splinters of ice through the hull with a noise like rifleshots. It became increasingly difficult to steer a straight course or to plot the ship's position.

Then, at 9:25 a.m. on May 25, with the *Italia* at an altitude of only 750 feet, the elevator wheel jammed in a nose-down position. As the ship began to dive toward the pack ice, Nobile ordered all engines stopped, and the descent was arrested at 250 feet above the ice. With its engines dead, the *Italia* now floated upward like a free balloon, rising above the fog to brilliant sunshine at about 2,700 feet. This gave the navigators a chance to take a sun shot and fix the ship's position: some 180 miles northeast of King's Bay. It also caused the gas cells to expand and blow off precious gas; when the ship came down below the fog again it would be dangerously heavy. After half an hour the crew had repaired the elevator wheel; Nobile ordered the engines started and took the *Italia* down again to prevent further loss of gas. The ship butted its way south between the frozen sea below and freezing fog above for another 30 minutes before there came a cry from the helmsman: ''We're heavy!''

The *Italia* was dipping at the stern and falling almost two feet per second. Nobile ordered all engines full ahead and attempted to raise the ship's nose, but the rate of fall was accelerating. A crash was unavoidable, and the men in the control car stared in horror as the jagged ice rushed up to meet them. "It's all over," Nobile thought.

When the *Italia* hit, the control car and stern-engine gondola were ripped from the hull, depositing 10 men on the ice. Suddenly lightened, the rest of the airship drifted away on the wind, with six men still on board. Of those on the ice, one had been killed and four injured; the most seriously hurt was Nobile, who had broken his right leg and arm.

For the nine icebound survivors the prospect seemed grim: The weather was bitterly cold, and the barren pack ice stretched away for hundreds of miles. But the uninjured men, rummaging in the wreckage around them, raised the party's hopes when they found some of the *Italia's* survival equipment, including a tent, a revolver and enough provisions, they figured, to last for 45 days. Most heartening of all, the emergency radio had survived the crash, and even before the tent had been put up the radio operator was tapping out a distress call—SOS ITALIA. NOBILE. . . . SOS ITALIA. NOBILE—for the *Città di Milano* at King's Bay. But no one heard him, because no one was listening.

The *Città di Milano* was equipped with receivers and a transmitter powerful enough for continuous long-range communication. Instead of keeping a constant radio watch once the *Italia* was overdue, however, the ship stopped monitoring. The radiomen were busy transmitting the crew's personal messages and journalists' speculative stories back to Italy. When a junior radioman did pick up one faint SOS, his report was brushed off. Later, Captain Romagna was full of preposterous excuses: He thought the *Italia's* radio equipment had been damaged, or that the radioman on board had been killed, or that the airship had perished with all hands. The captain's dereliction may also have reflected his knowledge that the regime in Rome had little interest in Nobile and his men. In Italy, in fact, it was widely assumed that they were dead.

On the ice, the survivors waited. Every day the radioman sent his SOS, and every evening the men heard the latest bulletins from Rome, including football scores and news of their own disappearance. Each day the situation grew more desperate. The drifting ice was taking them away from their base; in 48 hours they had floated 28 miles. On May 30, Nobile's two navigators, Adalberto Mariano and Filippo Zappi, grew tired of waiting and set out toward King's Bay to get help. Finn Malmgren, the expedition's only Arctic expert, went with them.

The six men remaining at the makeshift camp continued to hope for rescue, and on June 6 they heard the electrifying news that a young farmer in Russia had picked up their distress signal on his radio. A day later there was even greater excitement when a message came through that help was on its way; Nobile ordered the tent colored with red stripes of navigation marker dye so that search planes could see it more easily.

Seven nations sent men and machines to scout the Arctic for the missing explorers. A Norwegian search ship had reached King's Bay on June 4; by June 19 three Swedish rescue planes had arrived in the area

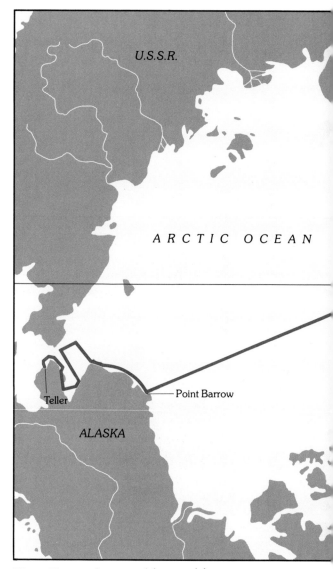

The red line on this map of the top of the world is the route followed by Amundsen and Nobile in the Norge, from King's Bay, Spitsbergen, across the North Pole to Alaska. The green line traces Nobile's subsequent flight in the Italia, from King's Bay via Greenland to the Pole, and thence to the site of his crash on an ice pack.

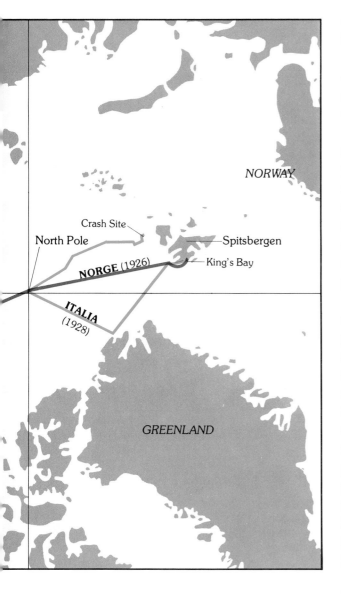

on board an aircraft-support ship. The next day the Russian icebreaker *Krassin* left Leningrad to take part in the massive search operation.

Even Roald Amundsen, burying his hard feelings, joined the crew of a French flying boat to search for his rival and fellow explorer. But after taking off from Tromsö, far north of the Arctic Circle, the plane was never seen again.

More flying boats continued to arrive at King's Bay. Two Italian aviators, Majors Pier Luigi Penzo and Umberto Maddalena, brought their planes to join in the search. On June 20, Maddalena, led by radio signals from the survivors' camp, approached the red tent at 300 feet, lost it, and then, beaming in on another signal, found it again. He dropped several packages containing such survival gear as radio batteries, shoes and smoke signals, along with eggs, marmalade and fresh fruit. Two days later both Italian planes flew over and showered the camp with parcels, including medical supplies, a stove and cigarettes.

The assistance was timely, for the sea ice was cracking and melting fast as the summer progressed and the tent was now surrounded by patches of water. The problem now was how to rescue the *Italia's* survivors before the ice disintegrated altogether. Later that day two Swedish seaplanes reached the camp, where they dropped more parcels—including two bottles of whiskey—and a message informing Nobile that one of them would try to land the next day if the survivors would mark a suitable site. Nobile's men laid out strips of red parachute to mark a relatively smooth spot of flat ice, and on June 23 the Swedish pilot Einar Lundborg managed to set his aircraft down while two other planes circled overhead. He had strict orders, he said, to rescue Nobile first. Nobile protested that as commander he should be taken off last. But Lundborg was insistent, and Nobile finally convinced himself that he would be more useful coordinating the rescue operation from King's Bay than lying helpless with a broken leg and arm on the pack ice.

The Swedes brought Nobile back to his base ship, the *Città di Milano.* He fully expected to return to the ice and take charge of rescue operations, but Captain Romagna had other orders, and other plans. On directions from Rome, Nobile was made a virtual prisoner in his cabin.

By July 3, nearly six weeks after the airship had gone down and two weeks after Nobile's rescue, no more men had been saved and it seemed that the tragedy was widening. The ice around the lonely red tent was melting dangerously, and the Swedish pilot Lundborg, returning to pick up others on the same day he rescued Nobile, had crashed on landing and was himself now a prisoner of the ice. The *Italia* had not been sighted since it had drifted away after the crash, and nothing was known of Mariano, Zappi and Malmgren, who had set out on foot for King's Bay. The rescue ships were ice-locked; Amundsen was missing and presumed dead. A Russian pilot was missing. And the Swedes decided that the ice at the campsite was no longer safe for airplane landings. On July 6 they managed to pluck Lundborg from the ice in a little Moth two-seater; then they withdrew from the rescue mission.

Only the Soviet icebreaker *Krassin* persisted in the search, and it was running low on coal. Making a mile and a half per hour through ice six feet thick, the sooty vessel plowed on, its decks crowded with lookouts. Then at 5:20 a.m. on July 12 a crewman cried out: "A man! A man! I can see him!" It was Filippo Zappi, still on his feet after 42 days of wandering across the ice, his face burned almost black by the sun. "*Krassin,* welcome!" he shouted as the icebreaker drew near. With him on a tiny ice floe, lying soaked to the skin in a pool of frigid water and unable to stand, was Adalberto Mariano. Finn Malmgren had died a month earlier, Zappi explained—he had just lain down in the snow and never got up again. (Persistent rumors would have it that Zappi's survival was the result of his having cannibalized his Swedish colleague.) Taking the two men on board, the *Krassin* continued its snail-like search until finally it neared the position of the red tent. Its siren whistling shrilly over the white wastes, the ship moored within 150 yards of the little camp where five men were still alive. The lost airship's radioman sent out his last signal: "It is over! *Krassin* is here! We are saved!"

Umberto Nobile's ordeal was not over. In the eyes of the government in Rome, the captain of the *Italia* expedition had lost his ship, abandoned his men and brought disgrace to Italy. When he and the survivors of his expedition disembarked from the *Città di Milano* at Narvik, Norway, and boarded a train for home, Nobile was dazed by the unfriendly mood of the Norwegian crowds, the hostile press coverage and the accusations of cowardice and incompetence that his own government had lodged against him. To be sure, once he reached Rome jubilant

Four weeks following the crash of the Italia, marooned crew members (left) signal to a plane dropping supplies. Above, a haggard Colonel Nobile, rescued from the ice pack, shares food with his dog, Titina. After three more weeks (right), the Russian icebreaker Krassin finally reaches the remaining survivors.

crowds numbering nearly a quarter of a million greeted his arrival, but he had been all but disowned by the official establishment. The Fascist press did everything it could to blacken his name—it was even suggested that he be tried by court-martial and shot, and an official inquiry, a kind of trial, was ordered. Seven months later, Umberto Nobile was formally held responsible for the loss of the *Italia.* With a peculiar twist of logic, the failure of his mission was judged to be a crime.

Dishonored at home, the 46-year-old Nobile eventually emigrated to the Soviet Union, where he designed several semirigid airships for the Russians. He returned briefly to Italy, but in 1939, just before the outbreak of World War II, he moved to the United States to accept a modest post at an aeronautical school in Chicago. Later, after the fall of Mussolini (Italo Balbo having been killed when his plane was shot down under mysterious circumstances early in the War), Nobile returned to Italy and worked to clear his name. In time he was vindicated, and the value of his polar achievements was recognized. When the American nuclear submarine *Nautilus* made its epic underwater crossing of the Arctic Ocean in 1958, its route was similar to that of Nobile's *Norge,* but in the opposite direction—from Alaska to Spitsbergen via the North Pole. Afterward, the submarine's captain wrote a letter of tribute to the aged Nobile, who was to live on until 1978: "From your courageous flight over the polar ice pack in 1926 it was established that there was no land between Alaska and Spitsbergen. Without this knowledge, found by you and confirmed by the aerial expeditions that followed you, we would not have known enough to undertake our voyage."

Majestic advent of a graceful colossus

Germany's *Graf Zeppelin,* launched at Friedrichshafen in 1928, was a proper monument to its namesake, Count Ferdinand von Zeppelin, the nation's revered airship pioneer, who had died 11 years earlier. Larger than any dirigible built before it—10 stories high and more than two city blocks long—the stately ship loomed over the crewmen who served it like some immense Gulliver over an army of Lilliputians.

Officially designated the LZ 127, it was affectionately called the *Graf*—at first in Germany and then everywhere as its reputation grew. From the outset, great things were expected of it. After the *Graf's* maiden flight, which lasted only three hours but passed without a hitch, the young American magazine *Time* predicted: "Certainly for transoceanic trips, the airship is the thing."

Indeed, the *Graf Zeppelin's* builders had intended to combine the range and unruffled comfort of a luxury ocean liner with—almost—the speed of a contemporary airliner. And, over nearly a decade of impeccable service, the *Graf* would rarely let its supporters—or its passengers—down. It would circle the earth, touch down on five continents, visit the Arctic and, in 1931, inaugurate the first transoceanic airline service, linking Europe and South America.

Before it was retired with honor in 1937, the benevolent giant had completed 590 flights and had logged 17,179 hours in the air. But its reputation rested more on style than on statistics. As one satisfied passenger said: "On a plane you fly, but on the *Graf* you voyage."

Nose first, the 3,707,550-cubic-foot Graf Zeppelin is guided on trolleys into its hangar at Friedrichshafen, aided by ground crewmen holding handrails on the gondola and many-stranded ropes called "spiders." The docking operation required between 300 and 500 men.

Disappearing over the rim of Wembley Stadium near London in 1930, the Graf Zeppelin is photographed at an angle that makes it appear to be diving.

Ohio, in 1933. This view, looking astern, shows the after portion of the Graf's passenger gondola and all five of its externally mounted engines.

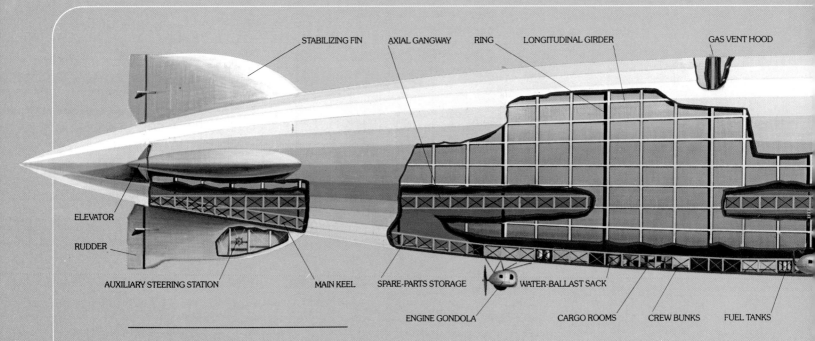

STABILIZING FIN   AXIAL GANGWAY   RING   LONGITUDINAL GIRDER   GAS VENT HOOD

ELEVATOR

RUDDER

AUXILIARY STEERING STATION   MAIN KEEL   SPARE-PARTS STORAGE   WATER-BALLAST SACK

ENGINE GONDOLA   CARGO ROOMS   CREW BUNKS   FUEL TANKS

A look inside the mighty Graf

The anatomy of the *Graf Zeppelin* at its launching in 1928 is shown in the cutaway drawings on these and the following pages. Designed by Ludwig Dürr, the *Graf* had dimensions dictated by those of the great shed at Friedrichshafen in which it was built. Critics pointed out that it was too slender for peak aerodynamic efficiency (a stouter shape would have permitted a smoother air flow). Even so, it was larger (3.7 million cubic feet), longer (775 feet) and had a greater diameter (100 feet) than any earlier dirigible; moreover, it could cruise at 73 mph and reach a top speed of 80.

Inside the hull was an intricate geometric pattern of rings, trusses and girders. The gondola *(right)* combined the ship's operating facilities with passenger quarters designed for comfortable long-distance travel. These accommodations featured a lounge, 16½ by 16½ feet, that doubled as a dining room, seating 16 persons at four tables, and a double row of 10 sleeping cabins, each with its own window on the world below.

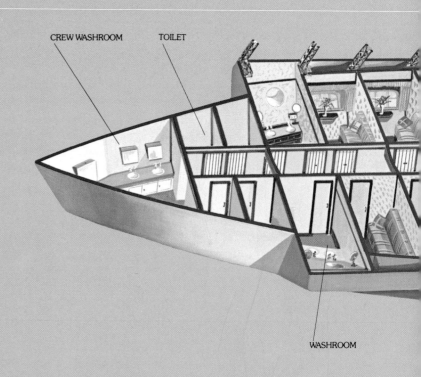

CREW WASHROOM   TOILET

WASHROOM

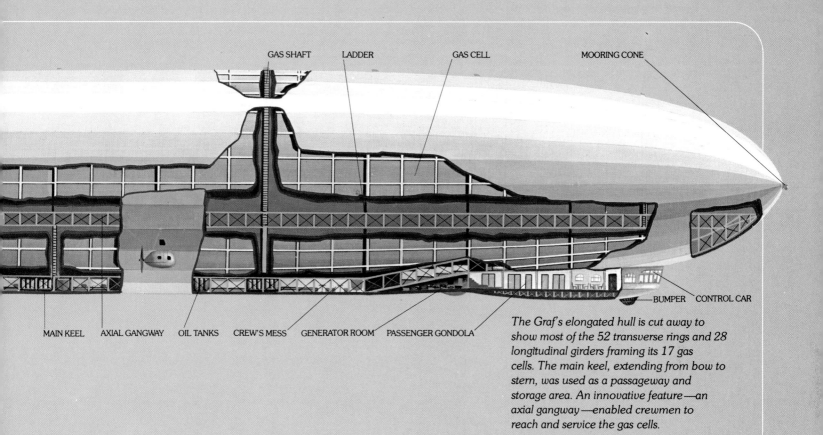

GAS SHAFT LADDER GAS CELL MOORING CONE

MAIN KEEL AXIAL GANGWAY OIL TANKS CREW'S MESS GENERATOR ROOM PASSENGER GONDOLA BUMPER CONTROL CAR

The Graf's elongated hull is cut away to show most of the 52 transverse rings and 28 longitudinal girders framing its 17 gas cells. The main keel, extending from bow to stern, was used as a passageway and storage area. An innovative feature—an axial gangway—enabled crewmen to reach and service the gas cells.

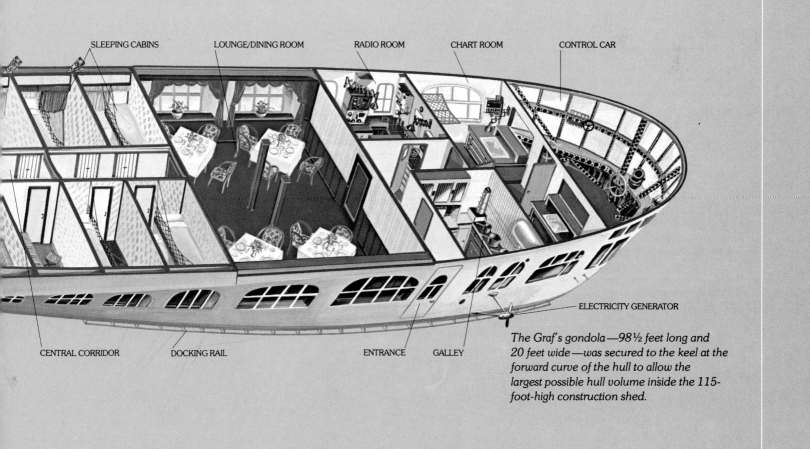

SLEEPING CABINS LOUNGE/DINING ROOM RADIO ROOM CHART ROOM CONTROL CAR

CENTRAL CORRIDOR DOCKING RAIL ENTRANCE GALLEY ELECTRICITY GENERATOR

The Graf's gondola—98½ feet long and 20 feet wide—was secured to the keel at the forward curve of the hull to allow the largest possible hull volume inside the 115-foot-high construction shed.

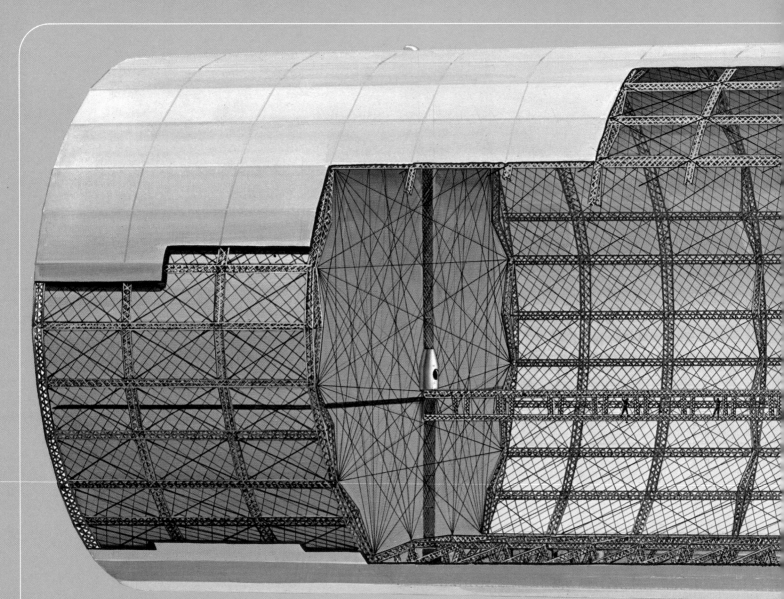

This cutaway reveals the hull's chief components. Each main ring, made up of 12 diamond-shaped trusses and held in place by a maze of steel bracing wires, was interposed at intervals of approximately 16 feet by two unbraced secondary rings; all were connected to longitudinal girders and, at the bottom, to the laterally braced keel. Gas cells (left) were contained in the bay between each pair of main rings, and excess gas was vented from a control capsule accessible from the central gangway.

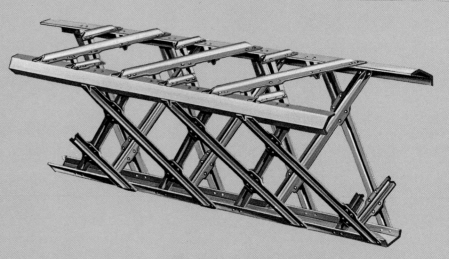

The Graf's structural members, assembled in a reinforcing crosshatch pattern, were made of duralumin, an alloy as strong as steel but only one third as heavy. Even so, the ship contained 33 tons of the metal.

A typical cell bay amidships on the Graf held two separate cells with a narrow walkway running through them. The upper cell contained hydrogen; the lower one contained gaseous engine fuel.

Each of the Graf's five 12-cylinder Maybach VL-II engines, in a pod large enough to permit maintenance during flight, could operate equally well on liquid fuel or a propane-like fuel called Blaugas.

4

Touring the world on "the ship with a soul"

On July 8, 1928, while the last survivors of the *Italia* were awaiting rescue from the arctic ice pack, Countess Hella von Brandenstein-Zeppelin mounted a flower-bedecked platform beneath the nose of a newly built passenger airship at the Zeppelin Company's factory in Friedrichshafen, Germany, and ceremoniously cracked open a bottle of fine champagne. As the only child of Count—the German word is *Graf*—Ferdinand von Zeppelin, who had died 11 years earlier at the age of 79, the Countess had been asked to christen the huge ship *Graf Zeppelin* in honor of her father. Fittingly, it was the 90th anniversary of the Count's birth; the German airship program he had pioneered had been reborn after several years of scratching to survive. The *Graf Zeppelin* would soon become the pride of a resurgent nation and a wonder of the world.

The spectacular catastrophes that had befallen the airships of several nations in the decade following the First World War had done little to dampen the enthusiasm of their dedicated advocates, some of whom still were looking forward to a golden age of intercontinental airship passenger travel. Nowhere did Count von Zeppelin's old dream glimmer so brightly as in his native Germany, where its cause was ably and eagerly championed by Hugo Eckener, who had been one of the Count's earliest disciples.

Eckener, having started 22 years earlier as an airship publicist and confidential aide, had moved steadily upward in the Zeppelin Company, and by 1922 had become its operational chief. He had never wavered in his belief in the future of long-range passenger airships, but his prospects had been considerably dimmed by Germany's defeat in the World War. The triumphant Allies, in addition to confiscating Germany's surviving military Zeppelins and banning the construction of new ones, had also limited the gas capacity of its commercial airships to one million cubic feet—far too small a quantity for a dirigible that could fly the all-important Atlantic route. Even at that, two commercial Zeppelins built not long after the Armistice were seized as additional war reparations, and the once-proud Zeppelin Company was reduced to manufacturing aluminum pots and pans in order to survive.

The company's fortunes took a turn for the better in 1922, when the United States Navy placed its order for the ZR 3—later named the *Los Angeles*. In 1924 Eckener himself flew the finished ship across the Atlantic for delivery to the United States Naval Air Station

Hugo Eckener, the driving force behind the resurgence of passenger dirigibles in Germany in the 1920s, stands near twin engine telegraphs at his post in the control car of the Graf Zeppelin.

at Lakehurst, New Jersey, and the rapturous reception he was given by the American people was surpassed only by the welcome he received following his return, by steamship, to his homeland. The highly publicized flight of the ZR 3 was viewed—not only in the struggling Weimar Republic but throughout the world—as a symbol of Germany's postwar resurrection; and Hugo Eckener became a German hero and an international celebrity.

But Germany still did not have a rigid airship of its own. Unless the Zeppelin Company could build another ship—one that would be large enough to demonstrate the possibilities of worldwide passenger airship travel—it would wither away. One obstacle was removed in 1925 when the limitation the Allies had imposed on the size of German airships was rescinded in the Treaty of Locarno. A problem of money, however, remained. Germany was in the throes of a continuing economic crisis, and neither the government nor the Zeppelin Company had the funds necessary for a major airship project.

Eckener hoped that German citizens might contribute to the cause as they often had to Count von Zeppelin's prewar appeals. He launched the Zeppelin-Eckener Subscription and, with his senior airship commanders, he stumped the length and breadth of the country on an exhausting lecture and fund-raising tour. After two years he had raised two and a half million marks; it was barely half the amount that the company required, but it was enough for Eckener to begin building his new airship. And once construction was under way, the German government agreed to put up the rest of the money.

The ship was designed by Ludwig Dürr, who had drawn the plans for all but the very earliest of the Zeppelins. At 775 feet long, 100 feet wide and 110 feet high, it was the largest one yet built, and with its heat-reflecting, aluminum-doped outer cover it looked like a great silver fish.

The *Graf Zeppelin* left its hangar for the first time on September 13, 1928, and a little more than three weeks later set out on the first transoceanic voyage ever made by an airship carrying paying passengers. On the morning of October 11, the dirigible took off from Friedrichshafen, bound for Lakehurst with 20 passengers and a crew of 40 on board. The trip was an experimental one, designed to demonstrate that passengers could be transported in comfort and safety over great distances at relatively high speed. Eckener, in command of the flight, decided against flying through the bad weather along the shorter great-circle route over Scotland and Labrador; he chose instead to show off the *Graf Zeppelin* along an extended southern route: Switzerland, France, Spain, Gibraltar and Madeira.

The newest Zeppelin, popularly called the *Graf,* was more comfortable than any that had yet flown. Its gondola, nearly 100 feet long and 20 feet wide, was palatial by the standards of the day, and its passenger accommodations aspired to the grandeur of an ocean liner. But the ship was really too small—and the first Atlantic flight too much an experi-

Breakfast takes wing, and passengers and crew members struggle to stay upright as the Graf Zeppelin is jolted by a violent updraft in this drawing made by one of the passengers on its first Atlantic crossing, in 1928. An excited journalist on board wrote that the ship "seemed to stand on its tail, with the point of its nose toward the moon."

ment—for all its backers' expectations to be instantly fulfilled. Everything on board had to be as light as possible: The temporary cabin "walls," for example, consisted merely of flowered chintz stretched from floor to ceiling. No one had anticipated the copious quantity of provisions that would be consumed on a long-distance passenger trip; as a result, first the bottled water ran out, then the wine, and before the flight was over the food too was almost gone.

The flight itself was uneventful until the third morning out. Just south of the Azores, as the passengers were having breakfast, the *Graf Zeppelin* flew at full speed into a threatening, blue-black wall of advancing clouds. Suddenly the bow dipped sharply downward; then, just as suddenly, it was hurled violently upward at an angle of 15 degrees. Lady Hay-Drummond-Hay, an Englishwoman representing the Hearst News Services (she was the only woman on board and was destined to become the first woman ever to arrive in the United States by air) described the "unutterable confusion" as chairs, tables and delicate blue-and-white Zeppelin chinaware crashed to the floor.

"Coffee, tea, butter, sausages, marmalade formed a glutinous mess and overspread the unlucky ones sitting with their backs to the stern," wrote Lady Hay-Drummond-Hay. "I in my chair slid the length of the saloon, crashing into the unfortunate artist, Professor Dettmann, who in turn fell over Robert Hartman's heavy movie camera, which fell full weight on Frederick Gilfillan. Breathless moments passed, leaving not a few blanched faces, and the thought—*we were facing death.*"

The turbulent storm front had torn off part of the ship's outer cover at the bottom of the port stabilizing fin, and the trailing strips of fabric threatened to jam the rudders and elevators. Eckener slowed to half speed as volunteers from the crew, led by Eckener's son, Knut, courageously climbed out onto the naked girders of the fin to cut away the trailing tatters and lash down the frayed edges of the cover.

On the next evening, after flying over Bermuda, the *Graf Zeppelin* ran afoul of a second storm. This time Eckener approached the front at half speed, but the *Graf* nevertheless dipped and rolled in the violent air currents as rain and hail rattled on the sides of the gondola, again alarming the passengers. But the following morning—beginning the fifth day out of Friedrichshafen—the *Graf Zeppelin* safely crossed the coast of Virginia near Cape Charles. After a triumphal flight over Washington, D.C., Baltimore and New York City, watched by millions of Americans whose interest had been stirred by radioed newspaper stories of the stormy crossing, the *Graf* moored at Lakehurst at 4:38 p.m. In 111 hours and 44 minutes it had flown 6,200 miles—the greatest nonstop distance so far covered by any aircraft. Hugo Eckener had remained at his post throughout most of the flight; in nearly five days he had slept only eight hours.

For all the public excitement that it generated, the *Graf Zeppelin's* first Atlantic crossing was only a moderate success. It had not really demonstrated either the comfort or the safety of commercial airship travel, nor had it shown any marked advantage in speed over the swift ocean liners of the day. Even so, Eckener and his men were feted wherever they went; they paraded up Broadway in a blizzard of ticker tape and had breakfast with President Coolidge in the White House. By the time they flew back to Friedrichshafen at the end of the month, the *Graf Zeppelin* was well on the way toward legend.

Indeed, there was a heroic quality to this silvery, slender leviathan. During the return flight to Europe the *Graf* ran into 75-mile-per-hour winds and was blown nearly 300 miles off course. At one time it was actually traveling backward at 18 to 20 miles per hour. But the *Graf* fought its way gamely to the French coast, proving that it could ride out the worst kind of weather the Atlantic could offer.

It was clear, moreover, that the ship bearing the old Count's name was capable—as he had been—of arousing extraordinary popular affection. Most of the people who flew in the *Graf* developed a feeling for it akin to that previously reserved for seagoing ships. Lady Hay-Drummond-Hay perhaps put her finger on the source of this appeal

Scattered over the landing field at Lakehurst, New Jersey, the hardiest of an original crowd of 50,000 await the Graf Zeppelin's arrival in the United States in October 1928. Slowed by fin damage over the Atlantic, the Graf arrived a day late.

when she wrote: "The *Graf Zeppelin* is more than just machinery, canvas and aluminum. It has a soul. I love the airship as if it were something alive, a being animated by life, responsive, grateful, capricious and lovable."

Despite the public acclamation, Eckener could not find the financial backing he needed to establish regular international passenger service. To keep his prized Zeppelin in the public eye he undertook a series of spectacular demonstration flights with influential government officials, politicians and newspaper editors on board. In late March, 1929, the *Graf Zeppelin* left a freezing Friedrichshafen on such a flight—a three-day, 5,000-mile, low-altitude cruise in the sun. The *Graf's* itinerary included the French Riviera, Corsica, Rome, Naples, Mount Vesuvius, Capri, Crete and Palestine. It was a luxury excursion. Over the Ionian Sea the passengers dined on turtle soup, ham with asparagus, roast beef, French cheese and German nutcake, which they washed down with fine wines and coffee. Over Crete they had breakfast and over Palestine lunch. They descended by moonlight to below sea level over the Dead Sea, cruised along the coast of Egypt, drifted past a snow-covered Mount Olympus, and then vaulted over the Dinaric Alps, negotiating dark, narrow passages and a driving blizzard to return home safely after more than 81 hours in the air.

A month later Eckener took the airship on a similar cruise over Spain and Portugal. These trips showed off rigid-airship travel at its most delightful—the views were incomparable, the service and cuisine first class, and there were few of the hazardous encounters with the elements that had beset the transatlantic flight.

Then in May of 1929 Eckener tried a second Atlantic crossing—and it nearly ended in disaster. When four of the ship's five engines failed over France, Eckener turned back. He was unable to make headway against a gale-force wind, and to avoid a crash landing, he had to ask French authorities to let him put in for repairs at an airship base near Toulon. After returning to Friedrichshafen on replacement engines, the ship was laid up for two months for modifications.

While the *Graf* was being modified Eckener went ahead with plans for his most ambitious excursion of all: a flight around the world. The earth had been circumnavigated by air once before—in 1924 four United States Army Air Service planes had set out from Seattle on a westerly course; two of them crashed along the way but the remaining pair succeeded in flying around the world in just under six months (the flying time had been about 15½ days), making 72 stops along the way. This considerable feat, however, led to no commercial or even military follow-up. With his projected flight, Eckener hoped to demonstrate that airship travel could be swift, convenient and safe, even on an extraordinary long-distance adventure. He also intended to obtain experience in airship operations in regions of the world where few aircraft, or none, had ever flown.

Eckener's main problem in mounting his expedition was financial—

A small enclave of boundless elegance

"You might easily imagine yourself on a ship with restricted quarters," said a traveler after a journey on the *Graf Zeppelin.* It was an illusion the airship's designers fostered in order to attract and satisfy customers who could afford the fare ($3,000 for the first transatlantic round trip, in 1928, reduced to less than $1,000 in the 1930s). The combination lounge-dining room was furnished with heavy wine-red drapes and carpeting, and the galley, though small, had the capacity to produce gourmet meals.

The luxury quickly won over most of the travelers. "We found ourselves in a pleasant room," one recalled, "getting acquainted over a midnight supper of lamb chops and peas, caviar and white wine. No steamship ever rode more evenly in a calm sea."

Despite occasional bumpings during rough weather, or disruptions in schedule, many of the pampered passengers returned to fly again, remembering that, as one of them wrote, even "the person with taut nerves may know a relaxation, a serenity and calm like none other in the field of travel."

The chef and his assistant prepare dessert in the Graf's galley. Their work was much appreciated because airship passengers did not suffer from motion sickness.

Ornate menus with commemorative illustrations, such as these from the Tokyo-to-Los Angeles leg of the Graf's world cruise of 1929, proffered a tempting range of hot and cold dishes.

LZ

ON BOARD
AIRSHIP GRAF ZEPPELIN
TOKYO–LOS ANGELES

SIXTH DAY
DINNER

Fillet of Anchovies, Pate de foie gras

Beef Tea

Cold "Kamakura" Ham

Asparagus Tips V

Cheese and C

Sand C

C

Imperial Hotel
TOKYO

THE GRAF ZEPPELIN
OVER TOKYO
THE IMPERIAL HOTEL

Above, passengers dine in an atmosphere of meticulous elegance. Table settings (right) of custom-crafted crystal, silverware and Bavarian porcelain (such as the sugar bowl below) bearing the Luftschiffbau Zeppelin initials were augmented by fresh flowers.

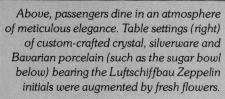

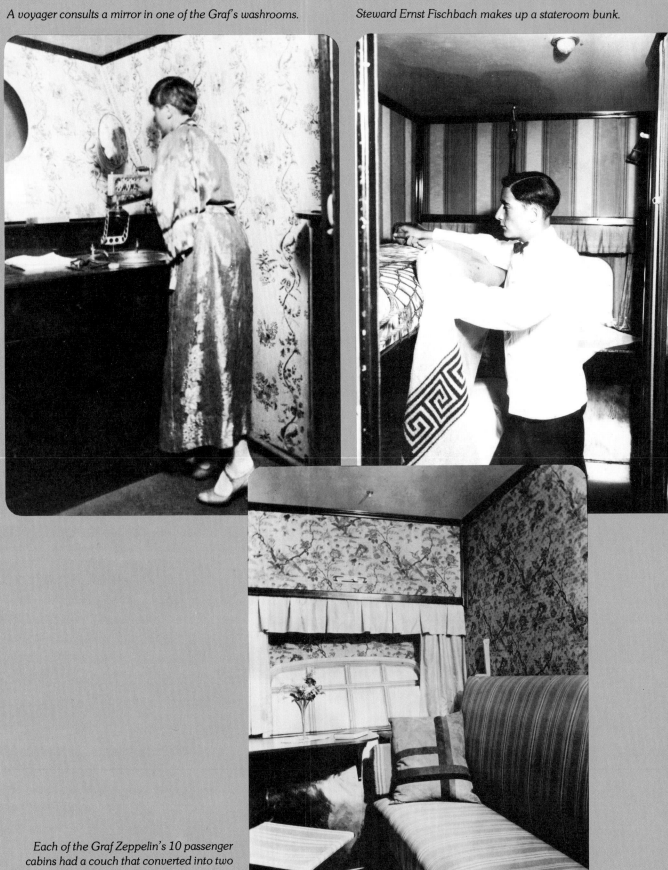

A voyager consults a mirror in one of the Graf's washrooms.

Steward Ernst Fischbach makes up a stateroom bunk.

Each of the Graf Zeppelin's 10 passenger cabins had a couch that converted into two bunks, plus a table, a folding stool, closets opposite the couch—and a view.

the cost of the flight was projected at a quarter of a million dollars. But this obstacle was cleared when several publishers, most notably the American press magnate William Randolph Hearst, advanced money in exchange for special coverage of the flight; the balance would come from a handful of paying passengers (at $2,500 a head) and from the sale of thousands of commemorative Zeppelin postage stamps that were eagerly sought by collectors. Hearst, who chipped in a generous $100,000, made an additional stipulation: As a condition of his support he required that the *Graf* begin and end its globe-girdling flight in America. Thus there would in effect be two eastbound world flights. The *Graf* would fly west from Germany to Lakehurst. Then it would fly east to start the American version of the world flight. It would land at Friedrichshafen and there start the German version. It would land again at the end of the flight at both bases.

The *Graf Zeppelin* duly arrived at Lakehurst on August 5, 1929, after a flight of 95 hours. There it took on several passengers, among them Lieutenant Commander Charles E. Rosendahl, captain of the *Los Angeles* and a survivor of the *Shenandoah,* and that indomitable Zeppelin fan, Lady Hay-Drummond-Hay, again representing the Hearst press. On August 7, the *Graf* took off and returned in just 55 hours to Friedrichshafen. Finally, at 4:35 a.m. on August 15, 1929, with 20 passengers (baggage allowance 50 pounds each) and 41 crewmen on board, the silver ship lifted off gently and the trailblazing stages of the great flight began.

Eckener had wanted to demonstrate how routine life could be on an intercontinental Zeppelin airliner. And indeed the passengers immediately settled into a routine that lasted as long as the voyage did; it was as if they had all been traveling around the world on dirigibles for years. The *Graf* had not been airborne half an hour before an American passenger had put a record on the phonograph in the dining room, and as the red dawn broke over Germany a Japanese journalist danced a solo Charleston. Photographers and movie cameramen scampered through the length and breadth of the ship and journalists tapped out their first stories in their cabins; other passengers turned their attention to card games, studied star charts, began diaries and scribbled postcards that accumulated into an impressive heap.

Over the Danube they flew, over Berlin, on toward East Prussia. As the passengers sat down to their first luncheon of Rhine salmon, saddle of venison, fruit and cream, the wine flowed and glasses clinked; towns and villages drifted swiftly past as the *Graf Zeppelin* drove at nearly 70 miles per hour toward the gates of Asia. At 6 p.m. the *Graf* passed the Soviet frontier and soon droned across immense open spaces where no aircraft had ever ventured before. "At dinner in the brightly lit ship," a German journalist recalled, "we forget everything, where we are, that we are going around the world, that we are setting course across Russia. We sit, eat, drink, chat and are cocooned by the roar of the propellers, whose clamor pours over the entire ship like a waterfall."

Summer nights are short in high latitudes and at four the next morning it began to grow light again as the sun rose over northern Russia. Peering from their cabin windows the passengers could see the golden cupolas of Vologda's 40 churches, then immense dark forests stretching to the horizon; peasants in the clearings fled in panic from the monster overhead. All through the day the ship thundered eastward, and shortly after midnight the *Graf Zeppelin* approached the Urals a little north of Perm, cleared their gently rolling, forested slopes with ease at 3,300 feet, and entered Asia. The forest gradually gave way to a vast and primordial marshland. Hour after hour the *Graf* flew over flat swamps that stretched to every horizon. Over such featureless terrain, devoid of any sign of human life, the navigators could hold to their course only by dead reckoning, using major river systems to take an occasional fix on their position.

As the *Graf* moved over the immense Yenisei River system, Eckener turned northward to find a village or town by which to determine his exact position. After an hour the ship rounded a bend and approached a collection of some 25 huts, which the navigator pinpointed as the village of Verkhne Imbatskoye. The unexpected appearance of the huge Zeppelin at low altitude was too much for the inhabitants of the remote village. Some ran into their huts and slammed the doors behind them; others remained rooted to the spot; domestic animals fled in every direction, and a horse galloped in panic down the street, flattening two huts with the cart it was pulling.

By sunset on August 17, the *Graf* was growling eastward over a steppelike plateau on the watershed between the Yenisei and Lena River basins. It was an extraordinary night. The full moon stood like an enormous yellow ball on the southern horizon while the sun hung just below the northern horizon and the sky glowed brightly with an uncanny luminescence. But it was desperately cold in the unheated cabins; when the passengers assembled for breakfast the next morning, they came clad in an assortment of heavy furs, motoring caps, camel's-hair coats and thick sweaters.

The *Graf Zeppelin* was now nearing Yakutsk, in northern Siberia. An ancient fur-trading post and place of exile on the five-mile-wide Lena River, Yakutsk was one of the least accessible towns in the world; the nearest railway station was more than 750 miles away, and the sea was nearly 1,000 miles away. The airship dropped down over the center of the town. Yakutsk was not much to look at—scattered log cabins, a few modest churches and government buildings, unpaved streets and log sidewalks. But after the empty wilderness of the last few days it seemed the height of civilization to those on board the *Graf*. Over the cemetery a wreath was tossed down in salute to the German prisoners who had died in this place during the World War, and the floral offering was followed by a mailbag stuffed with postcards for mailing to every part of the world.

Between Yakutsk and the sea one obstacle remained. The Stanovoi

Lady Hay-Drummond-Hay, chronicler and the only woman passenger on board the Graf Zeppelin during its global cruise in 1929, watches the world pass beneath her window in the airship's lounge.

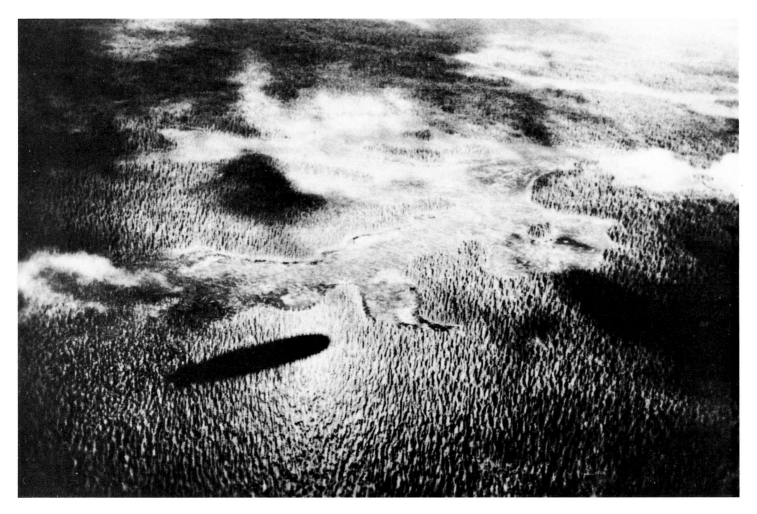

The shadow of the 775-foot Graf, photographed from the airship, glides over the densely forested swamps of Siberia. Even Captain Eckener confessed that he was glad to leave behind "that dread waste."

Range, running parallel with the eastern coast of Siberia, was for the most part unexplored and uncharted. Its towering ridges were said to average 6,500 feet high, but a 5,000-foot pass was believed to lead through the mountains to the Sea of Okhotsk. It was this pass that Eckener aimed for as the *Graf Zeppelin* drew near the mountains. The ship climbed steadily up a valley that became a canyon as it twisted and turned toward the summit. At 5,500 feet above sea level the pass still rose; Eckener was forced to take his craft higher and higher still, only a few hundred feet above the rocky ground, with the mountain crags closing in to within 250 feet on either side. At 6,000 feet the *Graf* was only 150 feet above the ground when at last the land began to fall away; the ship had cleared the mountains, and the men in the control car could see dead ahead of them the bright blue waters of the Sea of Okhotsk, which opened on the broad Pacific. Hugo Eckener, in a rare moment of public exultation, threw his arms in the air at the sight and exclaimed: "Now that's airship flying!"

Later that day the *Graf Zeppelin* traversed the eastern coast of Siberia, and Eckener turned the ship southward and set a course for the long leg to Tokyo. On the evening of August 19, 1929, after passing over wildly enthusiastic crowds in Tokyo and Yokohama, the *Graf* settled

Dwarfing the planes that have come out to greet it, the Graf Zeppelin cruises tranquilly over San Francisco Bay 67 hours after leaving Tokyo in 1929.

gently into the hands of a ground crew of 500 Japanese sailors at the Kasumigaura naval airship base. Nearly a quarter of a million people had gathered at the base to greet the aerial voyagers. They had covered the 7,030 miles from Friedrichshafen in just 101 hours and 49 minutes—an average speed of 69 miles per hour. It was a journey that would have taken more than two weeks by trans-Siberian railway and a month by fast steamer.

The Japanese gave the airship's passengers and crew an ecstatic four-day welcome, regaling the travelers with speeches, teas and banquets, and extravagant gifts. But Eckener was not able to enjoy himself. It was more than 100° F. in the shade, his uniform was hot and heavy, his socks had holes in them, the food was too exotic for his taste and he had a boil. He was anxious to be off in his Zeppelin, in the cool of the sky, across the wide Pacific.

When at last he got his wish, the flight across the North Pacific proved to be an uneventful one. Much of the journey lay through thick fog or solid clouds and the passengers could see little. After an ocean crossing of 67 hours, having gained a calendar day when the ship crossed the international date line, they arrived over San Francisco in the late afternoon of August 25. Squadrons of airplanes escorted the German airship over the Golden Gate, hundreds of ships in the harbor sounded their sirens and thousands of automobiles tooted their horns in salute. Making its way slowly down the California coast during the night, the *Graf* finally touched down at Mines Field, Los Angeles, at five the next morning, after a flight of 79 hours and 3 minutes from Tokyo.

On August 29, following a round of celebratory functions on the West Coast and a 52-hour, 3,015-mile flight across the United States, the *Graf Zeppelin* returned to Lakehurst. Its arrival marked the end of the American version of the world flight—which had covered 20,500 miles in a total of 12 days in the air. The parade up Broadway this time was even bigger than it had been after the first Atlantic crossing a year earlier; an estimated two and a half tons of confetti, ticker tape and paper scraps were showered over the visiting airshipmen as they passed. And at a reception at the White House, a new President, Herbert Hoover, was lavish in his praise. "I thought the days of the great explorers like Magellan and Columbus had passed," he said. "But now I see another great explorer, Dr. Hugo Eckener, standing before me."

Zeppelin Company business detained Eckener in the States, and his second-in-command, the veteran Zeppelin bomber captain Ernst Lehmann, took the airship back to Friedrichshafen. Navigating a somewhat longer course in order to take advantage of favorable wind conditions, Lehmann returned the *Graf* to its home base in 67 hours 31 minutes (averaging a swift 77.8 miles per hour), and the German version of the flight around the world came to an end on the 4th of September, 1929, amid music, confetti, bouquets, champagne and tumultuous applause. There was ample cause for excitement. In 12 days 12 hours and 20 minutes of flying time, the *Graf Zeppelin* had carried its passengers in safety and comfort for 21,376 miles, passing over regions that no human being had ever touched or traversed—or, certainly, had ever viewed from the air.

The *Graf Zeppelin's* circumnavigation had been watched with intense interest in England, where two immense airships were nearing completion. The British had revived their suspended rigid-airship program in 1924, following a vigorous two-year lobbying campaign by Sir Dennistoun Burney, a member of Parliament and onetime Navy commander who had made a name for himself during the World War with his invention of a mine-sweeping apparatus. He had devised an Imperial Airship Scheme as a means of linking such far-flung British possessions as Canada, South Africa, India and Australia to England with long-distance passenger and mail service.

Burney envisioned a fleet of six ships, but when the newly installed Labor Party government accepted his proposal at the end of 1924, the number was pared to just two. One, designated the R 100, was to be built by private enterprise; the other, the R 101, was to be a state-sponsored venture, intended as a monumental example of the virtues of public enterprise under the Socialist-leaning regime of Britain's Labor Party. Soon the R 100 became known as the "capitalist ship" and the R 101 as the "socialist ship," and an intense, often bitter competition developed between them. As one member of the R 100's design team, Nevil Shute Norway (better known later as novelist Nevil Shute), was to write: "The controversy of capitalism versus State enterprise has been argued, tested and fought out in many ways in many countries, but surely the airship venture in England stands as the most curious determination of this matter."

Both of the ships departed from the rigid-airship tradition in many design and structural details; both encountered numerous difficulties and were slow in the making. For the capitalist ship some of the first problems were environmental rather than technological. The old war-time airship station at Howden, where the R 100 was to be constructed, was infested with wildlife; the area was so damp that the construction shed regularly filled with mist that froze in the winter and coated the airship's girderwork with ice. There were no skilled workers in the vicinity, so the vast skeleton had to be assembled by local farm hands, hastily trained. Even so, the R 100 grew, and in its way it was an engineering triumph, with far fewer parts in its 709-foot-long framework than in any other rigid ever built.

In December of 1929 the R 100 flew from Howden to the proposed imperial airship base at Cardington, near Bedford, for preliminary testing. Then on July 29, 1930, with 44 persons on board, the ship took off on a major demonstration flight across the Atlantic to Canada.

Almost half a million pounds had been invested in the creation of the R 100 and it proved to be an excellent ship; sturdy and stable in flight, it exceeded its performance requirements with a top speed of 81 miles per

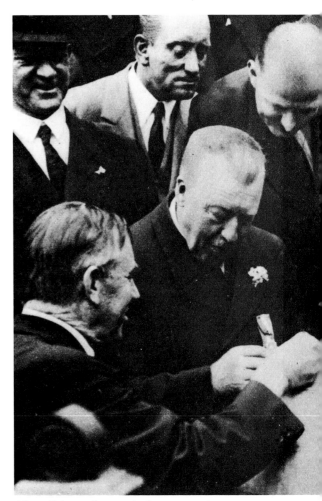

Hugo Eckener (wearing a boutonniere) traces the Graf Zeppelin's global route for a New York welcoming committee led by Mayor Jimmy Walker (far right).

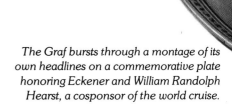

The Graf bursts through a montage of its own headlines on a commemorative plate honoring Eckener and William Randolph Hearst, a cosponsor of the world cruise.

hour and a useful lift of 54 tons. In addition, the passenger accommodations were outstanding. "The comfort of this flight is almost staggering," Nevil Shute noted in his diary. "Sleep all night in bed, get up, shave in hot water, dress and eat a normal breakfast served in a Christian way." The R 100 reached Montreal in a little under 79 hours and, after remaining there a fortnight as a tourist attraction, returned home on the prevailing westerlies in 57½ hours.

Now it was the turn of the R 101, whose demonstration flight was to be to Karachi (then in India) with a refueling stop at Ismailia in Egypt. But the government-sponsored airship was still far from ready for a trailblazing flight to anywhere. It was a beautiful ship on the outside and a palatial one on the inside, with passenger quarters on two decks that included a smoking room, a dining salon, a large gold-and-white lounge complete with potted palms, and a promenade with wide picture windows. But for all that, the 732-foot craft had too much about it that was new, and complicated.

During construction in the immense hangar at Cardington—the largest building in the British Empire—the R 101 had absorbed two miles of girders, six miles of booms, eight miles of struts, 11 miles of cables and 27 miles of tubing, all held together with 450,000 rivets. The 17 gas cells were enormous—together they would not have fitted into the length of Westminster Abbey; each one provided more lift than did the entire airship *Norge*, which had carried Amundsen and Nobile across the North Pole.

But the R 101 was overweight. The government had wanted it to be the best in the world, but the extra-strong stainless-steel-and-duralumin frame, the extra-safe diesel (instead of gasoline) engines, the extra-sure servomotors (instead of manual steering) combined to make it inordinately heavy; indeed, it had only 35 tons of useful lift, not the 60 tons that was desired. This would not be enough for regular long-distance flights in tropical conditions, where high temperatures would reduce the lifting properties of the gas still further. Moreover, the ship's novel gas valves were so sensitive that they leaked continuously.

In order to increase the airship's lift, the R 101's builders loosened the wire netting around the gas cells to enlarge their capacity. Unfortunately, the cells now chafed against the metal frame and they were perforated by innumerable small holes that steadily leaked gas. Moreover, the expanded cells were free to surge back and forth in the hull, which made the ship unstable and gave it a tendency to go into sudden, steep dives. The R 101 was not only heavy, leaky and unstable, it was underpowered as well, and its outer cover had rotted and split along the top and along one side.

Given time, most of these problems could have been solved. But the Secretary of State for Air, Lord Thomson of Cardington, had political reasons for wanting the R 101 put into service without further delay. Thomson had been a keen supporter of the Imperial Airship Scheme from the outset. He made a public show of concern about its safety, but it was rumored that he was more interested in his own ambition to become the next Viceroy of India, the most prestigious post in the British Empire. No doubt his chances would be vastly improved if he were to make a sensational arrival in the country of his ambition on board the majestic R 101. As early as November of 1929, Thomson scheduled the airship's great demonstration flight for the following September—which would give him just enough time to return in triumph at the height of air-service discussions scheduled to be held at the Imperial Conference in London in the middle of October. "I must insist on the program for the India flight being adhered to," he declared, "as I have made my plans accordingly."

The R 101 design team knew that if their ship was ever to reach India there was only one resort. They would have to cut the R 101 in half and insert a new gas bay to give the ship more lift. At the Royal Airship Works near Bedford, construction went ahead feverishly; nevertheless, the R 101 was not ready to fly again until the beginning of October 1930. Thomson chafed at the delay.

The R 101 had been given a new outer cover, its gas leaks had been remedied and its weight reduced. The new gas bay had increased the

One million visitors from Canada and the United States came to look at the R 100 during its 13-day visit to Montreal in August 1930. Here, some of them cluster at the base of its 200-foot mooring mast or wait for an elevator ride up to the ship itself.

ship's useful lift to a more satisfactory 49 tons and its length to 777 feet—two feet longer than Germany's *Graf Zeppelin.*

The British government's ship had become the biggest, costliest (£717,000) and most complex airship that had ever flown. It had not yet undergone final trials, but it was certified as airworthy on the condition that further tests be conducted en route to India. On October 1, the ship was brought out of its shed for the first time since being cut in two. The Director of Civil Aviation, Sir Sefton Brancker, protested the next day that the ship needed more trials, but Thomson refused to listen. The R 101, he had once said, was as safe as a house—except for the millionth chance. Now he intended to take that chance. Prudently, he also took out extra insurance for himself and his valet.

The officers and men of the R 101 and the Royal Airship Works had done all that could be done in the allotted time. The ship was not fully ready, but they still had confidence in it. Morale was for the most part high and the crew longed to be off at last.

Thomson allowed another day's delay to enable the crew to rest before the long flight to India, but the men spent the whole of October 4 loading and preparing the ship for its departure that evening; they were

The R 100's two-story dining salon could seat 50 people. At left, climbing a stairway to the mezzanine lounge, is novelist Nevil Shute, one of the airship's designers.

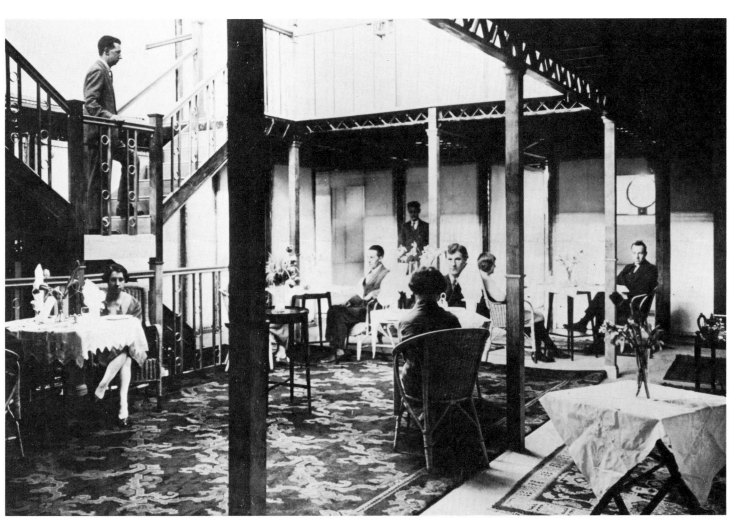

bone tired before they had even started. Still, exhaustion was the least of their worries. The weather was deteriorating, and by early evening a strong, blustery wind was blowing and the sky was overcast with low driving clouds. Moored to the Cardington mast 200 feet above the ground, the ship swayed gently in the gusts, its vast silver hull brilliantly illuminated in the beams of searchlights. Under ordinary circumstances the flight would have been postponed without question, but the R 101 was operating under extraordinary circumstances. The political pressure was so great that its departure on schedule was inevitable.

The authorities had seemed oblivious to the nature of the ship's predicament. The R 101 needed all the lift that could be had for its long flight through torrid climates, but the Air Ministry had nevertheless seen fit to add weight by laying a blue carpet down the length of the 600-foot-long corridor and over the floor of the passenger lounge, which was the size of a tennis court. "A layer of dust an eighth of an inch thick on top of the airship is said to weigh a ton," complained one of the ship's officers, "so you can imagine what *this* means to our load." Crates of champagne, barrels of beer and boxes of silverware for state banqueting had been brought on board; crewmen were limited to 10 pounds of personal baggage each, but Thomson's baggage was estimated to weigh considerably more than a ton. Some items were so heavy that two men were needed to carry them.

When the R 101 slipped from its mast at 6:36 that evening, it was so weighted down with baggage and extra fuel oil that instead of rising it sank slightly by the bow, and four tons of water ballast had to be dropped to get the nose up again. Sluggishly the ship moved off. The large crowd cheered, car headlights flashed on and off in farewell, and the R 101 glided out of the glare of the searchlights into the dark and the bluster of a gathering storm. For a while, pinpoints of light came from the ship as crewmen flicked their flashlights to signal good-by to families and friends. Then the big diesels roared to full ahead. "We're away, lads!" cried Chief Coxswain G. W. "Sky" Hunt, and the long-awaited voyage had begun. There were 54 men on board.

Over its hometown of Bedford, the R 101 dipped its bow in salute, then set course to the southeast at 1,500 feet and a ground speed against the wind of 25 miles per hour. But the slow-moving, heavily laden ship began almost at once to fall. A lady who was having dinner in her home near Hitchin, to the north of London, was startled to hear her servants screaming. "We rushed out—and there was the R 101 aiming straight for the house," the woman said later. "She was so low it didn't seem as if she could miss it. We could see the people dining, and the electric bulbs in the ceiling. She seemed to be going very slowly. As the green and red tail lights moved away up the drive, horror descended on us all."

The lumbering airship missed the house, and despite the fears on the ground, all was calm on board. The latest weather report predicted winds of 40 to 50 miles per hour—stronger than British airships had

Members of the British Parliament board the R 101 from its mooring mast in Cardington for an inspection tour in November of 1929. The problem-plagued R 101 was facing a major overhaul to reduce its weight and increase its lift.

ever encountered over land—but none of the ship's officers recommended turning back. At 8:21 p.m. they dispatched a routine radio message: "Over London. All well. Course now set for Paris."

In the dining room the R 101's distinguished guests, including the ambitious Air Minister Thomson, the Director of Civil Aviation, the Director of Airship Development and the airship's designers and top flight officers, sat down to supper. It was a cold night and it was a cold meal. But the passengers were relieved to be on their way at last—and they were hopeful of success.

The weather grew worse by the minute. Over the English coast at Hastings at 9:35 it was raining hard in a strong southwest wind; the ship pitched and rolled badly, causing the oversensitive valves on the surging gasbags to pop open and release precious gas with every movement. Ideally, a rigid airship always flew at an altitude at least 2½ times its own length. But over the Channel, with one engine temporarily out of order and rain water weighing heavily on the outer cover, the R 101 flew as low as 500 feet, only three quarters of its length, and crewmen could see the waves breaking in the windswept sea not far below. During the two-hour Channel crossing the ship managed to climb back to 900 feet, and at that altitude the first officer, Lieutenant Commander Noel G. Atherstone, took over the elevator wheel and brought it up another 100 feet. "Don't let her go below a thousand," he told the height coxswain as he handed back the wheel. But 1,000 feet was probably an average altitude on this flight, for the ship flew on an undulating corkscrew path, rising and falling by as much as 400 to 500 feet at a time.

At 11:36 p.m. the R 101 crossed the French coast near Pointe de St. Quentin, at the mouth of the Somme River. All seemed normal on board, and at midnight, while the ship was flying through intermittent rain and winds of 35 miles per hour, the radioman reported cheerily to Cardington: "After an excellent supper our distinguished passengers smoked a final cigar, and having sighted the French coast, have now gone to bed to rest after the excitement of their leave taking. All essential services are functioning satisfactorily. The crew have settled down to watch keeping routine."

With only 12 men of the watch still up, the R 101 battled across northern France into the teeth of the wind, its hull pitching and rolling, its gas cells surging wildly inside their mesh of restraining wires. To those watching from below, the ship again seemed perilously near the ground. Citizens of Quesnoy feared it would hit their houses; over St.-Valéry-sur-Somme people thought the ship was trying to land. Passing over high ground near the airport at Poix, it was seen to be down to an incredibly low 350 feet, less than half its length.

At 1:55 on Sunday morning, October 5, 1930, inhabitants of the town of Beauvais, 40 miles northwest of Paris, were roused from their sleep by the thunderous roar of engines as the R 101 passed over. Looking out of their windows they saw the dark mass of the airship drifting low overhead and wallowing in the wind; its red and green navigation lights glowed through the rain, and the lounge and cabin lights shone brightly, like the lights of a railway train in the sky. In the pitch darkness the 777-foot-long mammoth was pounding into a blustery wind of almost 50 miles per hour. At this point it was less than twice its own length from the ground, yet there was no alarm on board. The ship's watch was changed at 2 a.m. in a routine manner. Major George Scott, veteran of the R 34's trailblazing Atlantic crossing 11 years earlier, and the officer in overall charge of the flight, had gone to bed. The ship's captain, Flight Lieutenant Carmichael Irwin, went to his berth as well, leaving the watch officer in charge. As far as the crew was concerned, the flight was proceeding normally.

In the starboard after-engine car, engineer Joe Binks had just arrived, four minutes late, to relieve Arthur Bell from his spell of duty. Suddenly the ship went into a steep dive and both men were thrown off their feet. In the smoking room, where foreman engineer Harry Leech was puffing on a cigarette before turning in, the balsa-wood tables and wicker chairs began to slide toward the forward bulkhead and a soda siphon and some ashtrays fell off a table onto the floor. In the space of some two minutes the R 101 fell approximately 1,000 feet, coming very close to the rising ground beyond Beauvais. But the dive was arrested by the elevators, and for a short while the ship flew in a horizontal position— but with difficulty, as though it was becoming too heavy and sluggish to respond to the controls. Then it began to fall a second time.

The officer of the watch suddenly realized that a crash was inevitable. He signaled "slow" on the engine telegraphs, ordered a rigger forward to release water ballast by hand from the nose and sent coxswain Hunt to wake the captain and crew. "We're down lads!" Hunt shouted as he dashed through the ship. "We're down!" And indeed, in a few seconds the stricken vessel plunged to the dark earth. In the smoking room Harry Leech felt a great shudder run through the ship, and the floor and walls trembled violently. Then the ship's forward momentum was arrested with a jerk, and the lights went out. At less than five miles per hour His Majesty's Airship R 101 had struck the ground, bounced lightly and skidded forward for some 60 feet before coming to rest. It was nine minutes past two in the morning.

The nearest person to the point of impact was a rabbit trapper named Alfred Eugène Rabouille, who was preparing snares at the edge of a wood called the Bois des Coutumes. Rabouille had seen the airship coming low over Beauvais toward the only stretch of high ground in its path, a 750-foot ridge above the town. The ship was only 150 feet above the wood and only 250 yards away. "Suddenly there was a violent squall" Rabouille testified later. "The airship dipped by the nose several times, and its fore part crashed into the northwest edge of the Bois des Coutumes."

The French trapper then described the tragic moments that followed: "There was at once a tremendous explosion that knocked me down. Soon flames rose into the sky to a great height. Everything was enveloped by them. I saw human figures running about like madmen in the wreck. Then I lost my head and ran away into the woods."

As fire devoured the R 101, the windows of Beauvais were rattled by two more explosions. "It was as if the whole world had exploded," one citizen recalled. A huge fire lighted up the houses like a premature dawn. In the airship's mid-starboard engine car a vivid flash shot through the open door, scorching engineer Victor Savory's face and almost blinding him. In the after-engine car, where Joe Binks and Arthur Bell had been caught by the crash, Binks put his head out of the window and saw that the entire ship was on fire, the bare girders glowing with a fierce incandescent heat. Flames licked ominously through the floor of the car, but then a ballast tank burst overhead and doused them with water. Binks and Bell took this chance to escape, clambering out with their backs to the wind to protect their eyes from the flames. The immense hydrogen fire had consumed all the oxygen in the air around the wreck and the two men gasped for breath as they crawled away.

They had not gone far when they encountered a third survivor. Harry Leech, trapped in the smoking room, had torn his way out and jumped through the burning airship carcass, landing in the branches of a tree. "Come and help!" he shouted as rescuers ran up. "My pals are burning to death!" Then, although he was badly cut and burned himself, Leech raced back to the ship in order to try to save the others. But it was already too late. Only eight men had managed to get clear of the furnace that had once been the majestic R 101; of these, only six survived. The remaining 48—including Lord Thomson and all of the ship's officers—had perished in the fire.

As dawn broke, the skeleton of the ruined airship still flickered with fire as villagers and local firemen slowly picked their way through the debris searching for bodies. The dead, most of whom had been burned beyond recognition, were laid out under bed sheets at the edge of the wood, while the survivors were placed in the care of nuns in the local hospital.

The whole world was shocked by news of the spectacular disaster. A day of mourning was declared throughout France and its colonies. The town hall at Beauvais was temporarily designated "the Chapel of Repose for the Sons of Britain," and for two days the coffins of the victims lay in state there. When the time came for the dead to begin their journey home, more than 100,000 people crowded into the town to watch a procession of horse-drawn wagons file through the streets to the railway station, escorted by battalions of French infantry and squadrons of cavalry, and saluted by the firing of 101 guns.

All Britain was plunged into mourning. In London, half a million people lined the streets to watch the funeral procession, which was two miles long and took an hour to pass by. The dead were buried in a common grave at Cardington within sight of the two hangars that had housed the R 100 and R 101. No rigid airship ever flew again from these immense buildings. In a single crash—the worst disaster British aviation

A fire-ravaged skeleton sprawled across a wooded ridge in northern France is all that remains of the R 101 after its ill-fated voyage in October 1930.

French military units pay last respects to the victims of the crash of the R 101, whose remains had been brought by wagon to the railway station at Beauvais for the journey home to Great Britain.

had had so far—half of the nation's airshipmen had been wiped out.

The exact cause of the crash was never determined. In April 1931 a court of inquiry suggested that the immediate cause had been a sudden and massive loss of gas in a forward gas cell at a time when the nose of the airship was being sharply depressed by a downward current of air. It was possible that the turbulent head winds encountered by the R 101 over France had torn the outer cover at the top of the ship and exposed the gas cells in the bow to the fury of the elements. Structural failure was ruled out—though some critics maintained that the ship's back had broken at the point where the hull had been cut in half and lengthened. The reason for the fire was never exactly determined either. There were a number of possible causes—a spark from a fractured electrical cable, perhaps, a friction spark from the steel structure or a calcium flare in the control car, ignited by contact with water.

Criticizing the decision to begin the flight before the ship was ready for it, the court of inquiry declared: "It is impossible to avoid the conclusion that R 101 would not have started for India on the evening of October 4th if it had not been that reasons of public policy were considered as making it highly desirable for her to do so if she could." But no charges were made, for the men who were responsible had gone down with their ship.

The R 101 disaster set off a violent public reaction in Britain. "Ban the Gas Bags!" demanded the newspaper headlines. The Committee on National Expenditure advised against further spending on airships and the imperial airship program was abandoned. Its remaining ship, the successful R 100, was smashed to pieces with axes, flattened by a steam roller and sold to a scrap dealer for less than £600. ⌐⌐

Aiming high in Ohio

When the jointly owned Goodyear-Zeppelin Corporation of Akron, Ohio, contracted in 1928 to build two airships for the United States Navy, it first had to create an entire new industry. Hundreds of American workers had to be trained to work with imported German engineers, and thousands of patterns and procedures had to be perfected.

The streamlined hangar built at the Akron airport to house the project was a marvel in itself. Measuring 1,175 feet long, 325 feet wide and 211 feet high, the shed was so huge that it had a climate of its own; sometimes it rained inside. Eight of its 11 massive arches rested on rollers to allow them to expand or contract with changes in temperature. To reduce the air turbulence that could damage an entering or emerging airship, almost all corners and flat surfaces were eliminated and "orange peel" doors were designed to open flush with the contours of the building.

Work on the first airship, designated ZRS 4, began in 1929 and was the focus of constant public attention—and intermittent controversy. An investigation of sabotage (unfounded), charges of shoddy workmanship (untrue) and a report that the ship would be 10 tons overweight (true, but not serious) kept the project in the headlines. Even choosing a name for the new rigid was a point of argument until the influential local publisher John S. Knight suggested it be named for the city of its birth.

Yet for all the wrangling, as its launching finally neared in 1931 the U.S.S. *Akron* seemed to confirm its promoters' claim that "America now takes the lead in airships."

In the half-built hangar, 30,000 people watch Rear Admiral William Moffett (inset, with Goodyear president Paul Litchfield) drive a golden rivet to officially start work on the U.S.S. Akron in November 1929.

On the floor of the hangar, workers finish assembling one of the Akron's main frames. When it was completed, the 36-section ring was hoisted into a cradle for joining to the longitudinal girders.

The Akron's tail cone is hoisted into place to complete the 785-foot-long hull structure. The duralumin parts had been treated with aluminized varnish to prevent corrosion.

A mechanic (right) bolts on the massive nose spindle used to moor the airship to its mast. A panel of the cloth outer cover can be seen laced to the framework at upper left.

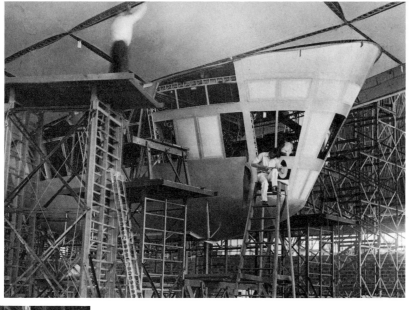

Workers finish mounting and equipping the control car. The spaces between the cotton panels (top) were reduced by lacing, then covered with strips of cloth.

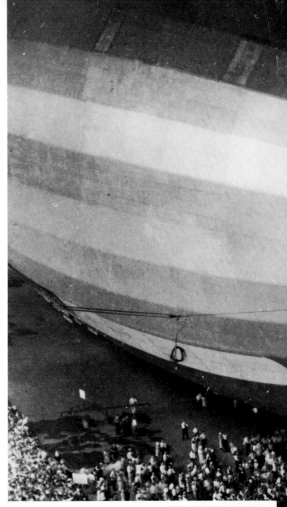

A quarter of a million people assembled on August 8, 1931, for the christening of the ZRS 4, described to a network-radio audience by CBS's Ted Husing as "the Navy's new battleship of the skies."

Mrs. Herbert Hoover (left) declares, "I christen thee Akron!" and pulls a cord to release 48 pigeons—one for each state—through a hatch in the ship's bow.

IN 2 TAGEN NACH NORD-AMERIKA!
DEUTSCHE ZEPPELIN-REEDEREI

5
Crescendo and calamity

With the abrupt demise of Great Britain's airship program, only two large rigid ships remained in service anywhere in the world—the *Los Angeles* in the United States and the *Graf Zeppelin* in Germany. In neither country did the R 101 catastrophe of 1930 have any substantial effect on ambitious plans for the airship's future. The Zeppelin Company went ahead with preparations to inaugurate the first scheduled transoceanic commercial air service, and took steps toward building a new super Zeppelin. The United States Navy commissioned the first of a new class of American-built military rigids.

The Navy's ZRS 4, better known as the U.S.S. *Akron,* was to be the biggest and most technologically refined airship the world had yet seen. The *Akron* had been in the planning stages since 1924. The crash of the *Shenandoah* in 1925 had aroused considerable opposition to the Navy's rigid-airship program, and all the persuasive powers of the Chief of the Bureau of Aeronautics, Rear Admiral William A. Moffett, were required to win approval for construction of another ship. Moffett had definite ideas about what the military mission of the *Akron,* and the ships he hoped would follow it, should be. "The rigid airship," he said, "is primarily a scouting ship, the purpose of which is to travel long distances at high speed, carry observers who can see what is going on and report back by radio."

In performing this mission, the new American airships would have a unique advantage over their predecessors: They were designed with room in their hulls for fighter planes that could defend the ship against an attack. So convincing were Moffett's arguments that a five-year plan, passed by Congress in 1926, called for the construction of two such rigids, ZRS 4 and ZRS 5. It also authorized the establishment of a new airship base on the American West Coast, and the construction of a small, experimental airship made of metal.

The Metalclad ZMC-2 was the first of the new ships to be completed and was immediately nicknamed "the tin balloon." Its hull consisted of riveted sheets of very thin, impervious duralumin that gave it a rigid form without the skeleton of girders pioneered by Count von Zeppelin. The helium that filled the single chamber of the Metalclad's interior was kept at pressure by ballonets, as in a nonrigid ship. The ZMC-2 first flew in August 1929 and would make 751 additional flights before being dismantled 12 years later because of old age. Yet it turned out to be one of a kind; the rest of the Navy's funds were committed to conventional

The new German airship Hindenburg, with Nazi swastikas prominent on its vertical fins, flies over the skyscrapers of New York in a 1936 poster that advertises regular passenger service on the largest and most opulent dirigible in the world. The poster promises "North America in Two Days!"

airships, and no other craft of its type ever got past the testing stage.

The construction of the ZRS 4 began late in 1929 at the huge new air dock erected in Akron, Ohio, by the Goodyear-Zeppelin Corporation, a partnership formed during the time when the German Zeppelin Company feared that harsh peace terms would bar it from ever again building large rigid airships. The Goodyear Tire and Rubber Company, headquartered in Ohio, was two-thirds owner of the joint venture.

Completed and duly christened in 1931, the *Akron* measured 785 feet long, with a gas capacity of 6,850,000 cubic feet. Designed for strength, it had three reinforcing keels to prevent a repetition of the mid-air breakup that had destroyed the *Shenandoah*. Eight inboard engines could drive this immense vessel at nearly 80 miles per hour. Its three fighter-observation airplanes were carried in a 70-by-58-foot hangar inside its hull and could be released and picked up in flight with the help of a special trapeze lowered through the bottom of the ship.

The *Akron's* ground facilities were as sophisticated as the ship itself. Newly developed equipment, including a movable mooring mast riding on railroad tracks, radically simplified the process of leaving and re-entering the hangar.

The *Akron* made its initial flight on September 23, 1931; its first captain was Lieutenant Commander Charles Rosendahl, who had survived the *Shenandoah* crash six years earlier. The Navy at last was equipped with a rigid airship specifically designed for fleet operations. The old German-built *Los Angeles* was decommissioned the following year, never to fly again, and it was contemplated that a total of 10 *Akron*-class rigids would eventually go into naval service.

During extensive journeys over the United States and on flights to Cuba and to Panama, the *Akron* experienced some minor difficulties, but its overall performance was satisfactory. Many old-line naval officers, however, doubted that an airship could be of much use in combat operations, especially since the development of aircraft carriers, which made any craft as big and relatively slow as the *Akron* a vulnerable target for enemy fighter planes.

Naval fleet commanders never employed the *Akron* on the long-range missions envisioned by Moffett, testing it instead in tactical exercises for which it was not suited—and indeed they were not impressed. At the same time a series of unfortunate incidents helped to diminish the *Akron's* reputation both with the Navy and with the general public. In one instance, a fin was smashed on the ground. Later, two line handlers who had been inadvertently carried up on the ends of their lines fell to their death; the accident was filmed by newsreel cameramen and widely viewed in the nation's theaters.

Then in the late evening of April 3, 1933, on a flight from Lakehurst with Admiral Moffett on board as observer, the *Akron* flew into a storm off the New Jersey coast. With lightning flashing all around and rain falling heavily in the black, windy night, the ship's new captain, Commander Frank C. McCord, headed east out to sea. He hoped to fly out

The principal movers of the United States Navy's airship program, Rear Admiral William A. Moffett (left) and Lieutenant Commander Charles E. Rosendahl, confer on the bridge of the Akron in 1932.

of the storm center, then circle around it and return to Lakehurst. But it was too late to escape the rapidly advancing storm. At 12:15 a.m. the *Akron* began falling rapidly; Commander McCord dropped ballast and set all engines at full speed. The ship leveled off at 700 feet, rose rapidly, then hit turbulent air and began to fall again at 14 feet per second.

McCord then ordered the elevator man to increase the rate of climb, and the nose came up by some 25 degrees, an alarming angle of ascent. At this point the altimeter in the control car read 800 feet. But in all probability the low barometric pressure within the storm had caused the altimeter to show the altitude as higher than it really was by at least 300 feet, and perhaps by as much as 600 feet. If this was so, the 785-foot-long airship had insufficient altitude in which to maneuver. In any case, with the *Akron's* elevators in the up position, its stern dropped and its tail smashed into the sea. The 200-ton ship hit the water at full speed and broke up. There was not enough lifesaving equipment on board for all, and only three men survived. The remaining 73, including Commander McCord and Admiral Moffett, perished in the freezing water.

The loss of both Moffett and the *Akron* resulted in a public outcry against further American participation in airship operations, and it was soon clear that the future of the airship in the United States depended entirely on the *Akron's* sister ship, the ZRS 5.

Only a few weeks earlier the ZRS 5 had been christened the U.S.S. *Macon* by Admiral Moffett's wife, in politically prudent honor of the largest city in the Georgia Congressional district of Carl Vinson, the powerful chairman of the House Committee on Naval Affairs. Like the *Akron,* the *Macon* would be consistently misemployed. During maneuvers with the Pacific Fleet in 1933 and 1934 it was repeatedly "shot down" in tactical combat exercises for which it was neither intended nor suited. Further unsatisfactory exercises in the Caribbean led the Commander in Chief of the United States Fleet, Admiral David F. Sellers, to report that the *Macon* had "failed to demonstrate its usefulness." Sellers concluded that "further expenditure of public funds for this type of vessel is not justified."

Even criticism from such a powerful quarter did not put an end to the *Macon's* flying, however. Properly used, not in battle but as the aloof, all-seeing eyes of the fleet, the *Macon*—using its fighter planes as scouts—could cover as much as 129,000 square miles of ocean in a day, and there was talk of having it patrol the Pacific as far as Pearl Harbor in Hawaii. Meanwhile, the huge ship continued its training flights.

On February 12, 1935, off Point Sur, California, on its 55th flight and under the command of Lieutenant Commander Herbert V. Wiley, one of the *Akron* survivors, the *Macon* was struck by a heavy gust of wind. Severe turbulence on an earlier transcontinental flight had revealed a weakness in the hull structure at the point where the fins were attached; work on reinforcements had been begun but not completed. Now the upper fin was wrenched from the hull by the gust, deflating the gas cells in the tail cone. So much ballast was let go to compensate for the resulting heaviness of the stern that the ship rose far above its pressure height, and gas was vented through the automatic valves in such quantities that there soon was no hope of keeping the *Macon* in the air. Twenty-four minutes after the accident to the fin, the ship fell into the sea and slowly sank. This time the water was warm, help was at hand and only two of the 83 crewmen lost their lives. But the loss of the *Macon* was decisive. The public thought airships were dangerous, the Navy thought them useless, and America washed its hands of them.

With the crash of the *Macon,* Germany's *Graf Zeppelin* was the only active rigid airship left in the world, and people of other nations often wondered why the Germans had been so successful where all others had failed. The answer lay partly in the vast knowledge and skill the Germans had acquired in the construction and handling of more than 100 big rigids and in the caution and thoroughness with which they put this experience to work. The rest of the answer lay in the complex and commanding personality of Hugo Eckener.

Eckener was a master airshipman, economist, psychologist, journalist, scholar, publicist and world traveler. He was also a difficult man to get along with; he did not suffer fools gladly and was brusque and impatient with subordinates. On his Zeppelins he ran a taut ship and maintained strict formality in his relationship with his officers, but his stamina and brilliance inspired the unquestioning confidence of all who

At near-stalling speed, two Curtiss F9C-2 Sparrowhawk biplanes fitted with skyhooks approach the newly commissioned U.S.S. Macon over New Jersey in July 1933 to practice hooking onto the dirigible's trapeze.

Cleared by a green flag, the lead pilot hooks his plane onto the trapeze. As soon as the wishbone-shaped saddle (protruding from the trapeze) was lowered to steady the fuselage, the plane was lifted into the ship.

served with him. In the control room he was capable of alert concentration for hours on end and could remain on duty for several days if circumstances demanded. Moreover, he had an uncanny gift for reading the weather signs in the sky; he could sniff out a thunderstorm, find the weak spot in a squall front and predict the behavior of his ship in the differing air masses in which it floated. It was this kind of feeling for the air that kept Eckener and a few men like him in pursuit of the airship dream while the others dropped out of the chase.

In 1931, the year that witnessed the maiden flight of the ill-fated *Akron,* the *Graf Zeppelin* made the last of its spectacular demonstration flights—venturing far north of the Arctic Circle—and the first of its commercial passenger runs to South America. The Arctic flight was a scientific and exploratory venture to the little-known islands of Severnaya Zemlya and Novaya Zemlya, north of the Siberian land mass. The original impetus for the flight had come from an eminent Norwegian explorer, Fridtjof Nansen, who in 1926 had founded the International Association for Exploring the Arctic by Means of Airships, sometimes called Aeroarctic. Nansen had aroused Hugo Eckener's interest in the possibilities of using the *Graf Zeppelin* for polar exploration, and when Nansen died in 1930 Eckener succeeded him as president of Aeroarctic. In July of that year, the *Graf Zeppelin* made three forays to the Far North to gain experience in arctic flying; then on July 26, 1931, the *Graf* left Leningrad for the start of its polar expedition.

On board were 46 men—a crew of 31 plus a dozen scientists from four countries, two journalists (including writer Arthur Koestler) and a cameraman. To accommodate all the scientific equipment, supplies and survival gear—which included 12 tents, 23 sledges and several collapsible boats—the passenger quarters of the *Graf* had been considerably modified; scientific instruments filled the cabins, and the men slept along the keel. Eckener himself commanded the airship; Professor Rudolf Samoilovich, who had led the Russian rescue of the *Italia* survivors in 1928, headed the scientific party. The scientists had three goals: to record changes in the earth's magnetic field at high latitudes, to make high-altitude meteorological observations using radio balloons released from the ship and to explore and photograph unknown lands.

The *Graf Zeppelin's* route took it first to the northern Russian port of Archangel, and then, during the first evening of the flight, across the Barents Sea toward Franz Josef Land. The next afternoon the *Graf,* using inflated rubber pontoons, made a remarkable landing on the sea to rendezvous with a Russian icebreaker and exchange sacks of mail for the benefit of philatelists who had helped to sponsor the expedition. On board the icebreaker to observe the *Graf's* progress was Umberto Nobile, who had piloted the ill-fated *Italia* three years earlier and who would soon be advising the Soviet government on airship affairs. But the meeting did not last long, for the airship began drifting toward an ice floe; after less than an hour Eckener took off and headed east.

Early the next morning the north cape of Severnaya Zemlya came

into sight; for six hours the *Graf Zeppelin* cruised down its coast, mapping with panoramic cameras and making the discovery that Severnaya was not one island, but two. The ship crossed the Siberian coast over the Taimyr Peninsula and after surveying Lake Taimyr—which turned out to be much longer than it appeared on existing maps—set out to sea again from the mouth of the Yenisei River. It reached and photographed the northern end of Novaya Zemlya island to complete its scientific program, then turned for home. When the *Graf Zeppelin* reached Friedrichshafen early on July 31 it had covered 8,250 miles in five days, and had brought back valuable new information about the Arctic's atmosphere and geography.

Within the month, Eckener launched the *Graf* on the first of the year's three passenger flights to Brazil, the first scheduled transoceanic flights ever. The 1931 flights ended at Recife, in the state of Pernambuco, on the protruding northeastern tip of Brazil, where an airship mast had been erected. From there, passengers were flown to Rio de Janeiro, which as yet had no airship facility, by the German Condor airline. From the first, the flights were highly successful, and many more were scheduled: nine in 1932, another nine in 1933, twelve in 1934 and sixteen in

A contemporary painting shows the Graf Zeppelin approaching the Russian icebreaker Malygin off the coast of Franz Josef Land in 1931 for a ceremonial exchange of 50,000 pieces of mail.

1935. From the end of 1932 all flights went on from Recife to Rio, and sometimes stopped at Seville in Spain on the way back to Germany.

The service was especially popular among members of the large German-speaking colony living in Brazil, who were happy to pay the equivalent of $460 for a one-way ticket. In comfort and service the *Graf* had improved considerably since its pioneering transatlantic flight of 1928. The old-fashioned plush interior had been modernized, and the crew became so adept at the ocean crossing that hazards and setbacks were few. The ship kept to schedule so punctually that the citizens of Recife, it was said, could set their watches by its arrivals and departures.

Few voyages could be more pleasant than flying down to Rio on this wonderful ship: droning low across France and the Mediterranean and out over the broad expanse of ocean via the Canary Islands, past the Cape Verde Islands, through the tropics to Brazil's palm-lined beaches and Rio de Janeiro's incomparable vista of sand, forest and mountains.

In time, the *Graf Zeppelin's* flights became so routine that the citizens of Rio hardly bothered to look up when the great ship throbbed over. But there were always exciting moments for those on board. On one trip, five captive monkeys escaped and clambered jibbering high among the girders inside the ship's hull. During a local revolution in Brazil in 1935, the *Graf* was obliged to cruise up and down the coast for three days while loyal troops fought to regain control of the airship base at Recife; crewmen replenished the ship's supplies of meat and potatoes by hovering over a passing steamer and lowering a net to haul them in.

At the *Graf's* low cruising altitude—usually about 1,000 feet—there was always something to see: schools of flying fish; four-masters under full canvas; the cheering convicts of Fernando de Noronha, the Brazilian island penal colony that served as a navigational landmark after the long ocean crossing; and, on the mainland, jungle villages and plantations of cotton and cane.

The *Graf Zeppelin's* great initial success as a passenger vessel inspired Hugo Eckener to build a new dirigible to supplement his tiny fleet of one. Indeed, since the end of the World War he had dreamed of building the perfect airship, one that would incorporate all the Zeppelin Company's decades of experience, and that in size, speed, safety, comfort and economy could offer an attractive scheduled passenger service on the potentially lucrative North Atlantic run between Europe and the United States. A preliminary design for such a ship was canceled following the burning of the British R 101, and in its place work began on a craft that would be inflated with helium, which Eckener hoped to obtain from the United States. The new ship was designated the LZ 129, but would be known as the *Hindenburg,* in honor of Field Marshal Paul von Hindenburg, the revered German war hero who had become President of the Weimar Republic.

The *Hindenburg's* dominant characteristic was its size. At 803 feet it was four fifths as long as the *Queen Mary,* then the largest ocean liner afloat. Its 135-foot diameter made it much fatter than the elongated

At an airfield edged with palm trees in Recife, Brazil, the Graf awaits refueling in 1934. The inset poster shows its route to South America.

Graf Zeppelin, and thus more resistant to bending forces, and more efficient, for it contained more gas in proportion to its structural weight. Though only about 30 feet longer than the *Graf,* it had a gas capacity of more than seven million cubic feet, almost double the *Graf's* volume. The *Hindenburg* differed from the older ship in other important respects too. Its four engines were diesels, efficient, powerful, lightweight models developed by Daimler-Benz, with huge 20-foot wooden propellers. The passenger accommodations were housed entirely inside the hull and provided room for 50 people to travel in a spaciousness and luxury unmatched by any other aircraft. This aerial leviathan, incorporating the most advanced technology then available to airship engineers, had a range of 11,000 miles and a cruising speed of 84 miles per hour.

Work on the *Hindenburg* had begun in the autumn of 1931 under the supervision of Eckener's son, Knut. It was anything but an auspicious time to undertake such an immense project, for Germany was in a state of political and economic collapse; as government funds for the new ship dwindled, progress came almost to a halt. Then the appointment of Adolf Hitler as Chancellor of Germany in January 1933 gave the project new life. The Nazi elite had no love for airships, which they considered to have no military use in war, but Dr. Joseph Goebbels, the Minister of Propaganda and Popular Enlightenment, was quick to see the potential of Eckener's Zeppelins for spreading Nazi propaganda. In the summer of 1934 he contributed $500,000 of his Ministry's funds to the Zeppelin Company to speed up completion of the *Hindenburg.*

Unfortunately for Eckener—an outspoken anti-Nazi who was spared from the concentration camps only because of his world stature—this infusion of funds led to the virtual take-over of the Zeppelin Company by the state. In 1935 the Air Ministry formed the Deutsche Zeppelin Reederei (The German Zeppelin Airline Company), of which the state-owned German airline, Lufthansa, had 50 per cent of the stock; the old Zeppelin Company became a minority partner. The Air Ministry pumped another two million dollars into the *Hindenburg* project and appointed Eckener's right-hand man, Ernst Lehmann, as technical manager and superintendent of flight, with Eckener as a figurehead chairman of the board. Not long afterward the center of commercial flight operations was moved from Friedrichshafen to the new Rhein-Main airship port near Frankfurt.

When Eckener's dream ship finally emerged from its hangar early in March 1936, its 100-foot-high vertical fins were emblazoned with black swastikas set in a white circle against a vivid red background—the emblem of the new regime. And barely three weeks after its maiden ascent the *Hindenburg* was set to work by the government. In company with the *Graf Zeppelin,* already decorated with swastikas, the new ship flew from one end of Germany to the other, dropping leaflets urging voters in a nationwide referendum to support Hitler's remilitarization of the Rhineland. Eckener roundly criticized his colleague Ernst Lehmann for the younger man's eagerness to get the *Hindenburg* aloft for what

Intricate spider webs of wire restrain a gas cell (rear) that has been inflated for testing, in this 1935 photograph of the Hindenburg under construction. An axial corridor girder (upper left) ran through a tunnel in the gas cells, providing access to the cells and their valves.

Eckener called "this mad flight." Hearing later of Eckener's remarks, Goebbels flew into a rage and declared: "Dr. Eckener has alienated himself from the nation. In the future his name may no longer be mentioned in newspapers, nor may his picture be further used."

Eckener retained his post as chairman, however, and the Nazi government's doubts about his loyalty did not affect the status of the *Hindenburg,* which took off from Frankfurt on its first passenger flight—a round trip to Rio—on March 31, 1936. Two engines malfunctioned during the trip, but otherwise everyone was delighted with its excellent performance and luxurious accommodations. The ship was essentially faultless except in one crucial respect—it was not filled with nonflammable helium, as Eckener had intended, but with hydrogen. The export of helium gas from the United States was forbidden by law and Eckener's efforts to make special bilateral arrangements for its use in the *Hindenburg* failed.

Eckener had visited President Franklin D. Roosevelt at the White House in February to request permission for regular use of landing and hangar facilities at the Lakehurst airship base. Roosevelt acceded and the ship was scheduled for 10 round-trip flights between Frankfurt and Lakehurst in 1936, as well as six more flights to Rio. On each of its 10 flights to the United States, the *Hindenburg,* commanded by Lehmann, exerted such an appeal on the flying public that the ship was fully booked with 50 passengers on all 20 of these crossings. For Eckener, this represented the victory of the Zeppelin concept for which he had fought so long. In 1936 no other form of transport could carry passengers so swiftly, so reliably and so comfortably between two distant continents. The 1,006 passengers who flew the North Atlantic in the *Hindenburg* during that halcyon year enjoyed passenger flight in a manner such as no one had enjoyed before—or since.

The *Hindenburg*'s average time was 65 hours out to America and 52 hours back to Germany, and its routine was much the same from flight to flight. Travelers from Europe were bused from Frankfurt to the Rhein-Main airport on the evening of departure, and usually boarded while the ship was still inside its hangar. Travelers from America were flown down to Lakehurst from Newark airport by DC-3 aircraft and boarded while the ship was moored to its mast. The passengers got on by climbing retractable stairs lowered to the ground from the belly of the ship; at the top of the steps they entered B deck in the bottom of the hull. From there a flight of stairs to port and another to starboard led to A deck with its 25 double-berth cabins. Each cabin measured about five by six and a quarter feet; each was furnished with a wardrobe, a folding writing table, a folding stool and a folding washstand with hot and cold running water. Cabins were ventilated by forced air that could be warmed by hot water from the engine radiators.

The cabins were comfortable, functional and quiet, but the ship's designers had assumed that most passengers would spend their waking moments in the ship's public rooms and had accordingly built these on a scale unprecedented in any aircraft. The largest of them were outboard of the passenger accommodations on A deck. To port was the dining room, measuring 15 by 50 feet and with seating for 34 passengers. The tables and the red upholstered chairs were made of tubular aluminum and were so light that they could be lifted with one finger. Outboard of the dining room stretched a promenade deck 50 feet long, with wide sloping picture windows that provided breathtaking views and were often left open during warm weather. The inboard dining-room walls were decorated with specially commissioned murals showing scenes from the *Graf Zeppelin's* flights to South America.

The starboard side was occupied by a lounge 34 feet long and a writing room 16 feet long. The lounge was furnished with tables and chairs upholstered in rust brown and with an aluminum baby grand piano that weighed 397 pounds and was finished in yellow pigskin. A large chart of the world decorated the lounge wall, and on it were depicted some of the great ships of sea and air and their voyages—those of Columbus, Vasco da Gama, Magellan, Cook, the *Los Angeles* and the *Graf Zeppelin.* The writing room was fitted with pneumatic letter tubes leading to the mail room. On the outside of these rooms was another promenade deck, identical to the one flanking the dining room.

Below, on B deck, were a roomy electric-powered galley, the toilets, washrooms and shower room—and a smoking room that was one of the *Hindenburg's* outstanding features. Measuring 12½ by 15½ feet, it was made hydrogenproof by pressurization and an air-lock seal. One electric lighter, secured by a chain, was available for cigarette smokers; a steward would light a match for cigar and pipe smokers, but no passenger was allowed to strike a match himself or leave the room with matches or any smoking materials. The same steward also mixed drinks at a small bar that specialized in the "LZ 129 Frosted Cocktail," made from a little orange juice and a lot of gin. The other public rooms generally closed at 11 p.m., but the smoking room and its bar stayed open into the early hours of the morning; on one memorable occasion four merrymakers caroused their way through 15 bottles of Moselle by 4 a.m. Ensconced in this cozy little den, with its balloon and airship murals, the *Hindenburg's* convivial passengers could view the earth below from the most enviable perch imaginable—they could look straight down through windows set into the bottom of the ship.

The *Hindenburg* usually took off in the calm of the evening, and rose so silently and with so little sense of motion that the passengers often had no idea they were airborne until they noticed the apparently decreasing size of people and buildings on the ground. The ship was amazingly stable, and the Zeppelin Reederei's brochure boasted that "No passenger on any Zeppelin has *ever* suffered from airsickness." Indeed, pitching and rolling were barely perceptible, and turbulent air and gale-force winds that would have buffeted an airplane did not seem to create the least tremor in the *Hindenburg.* The vibration of the engines was not sufficient to ripple the surface of a glass of water in the

A brotherhood of dedicated captains

These five men, along with their charismatic leader, Hugo Eckener, commanded the *Graf Zeppelin* or the *Hindenburg* or both. More than seasoned and reliable captains, they were single-minded apostles of the airship cause. Together, they brought Germany's commercial airship service to full stride in the mid-1930s, extending safe, regular passenger service to three continents.

Senior among them was Lehmann, regarded fondly by both passengers and crewmen for his serene competence, his ready smile and the music he entertained them with: folk songs on his accordion, classics on the *Hindenburg's* piano. Recruited by Eckener in 1913, Lehmann succeeded him in 1935 as director of Zeppelin operations.

Like Lehmann, his fellow captains had served in airships in World War I (Max Pruss took part in 15 raids on Britain; Hans Flemming set an all-time airship altitude record of 24,000 feet while evading aircraft). What a colleague later said of Lehmann applied to each of them: "His whole existence was bound up in a great ideal—the perfection of airships."

passenger quarters or upset a pencil standing on its end on a table, and the noise level in the passenger accommodations was less than on any other form of powered transport of the time.

The days aloft were structured around meals served on stiff white tablecloths set with freshly arranged flowers, silver cutlery and ivory porcelain especially designed for the *Hindenburg.* The meals, served in two sittings, were sumptuous—a day's fare might include duckling for lunch, sole followed by venison for dinner, Moselle and Rhine wine and German champagne, or vintage wines from France. When not dining, the passengers passed the time staring out at the passing scenery, making friends, playing chess and cards, smoking and drinking, reading or listening to a fellow voyager play the piano. On at least one occasion Mass was celebrated by a Catholic priest on board, the first time that

ERNST LEHMANN

HANS VON SCHILLER

HANS FLEMMING

ANTON WITTEMANN

MAX PRUSS

such a service had been conducted in the air; the sacramental candles were kept safely unlit, however.

The *Hindenburg's* crew might number anywhere from 50 to 60, including 10 to 15 men in the stewards' section. Quartered in wardrooms along the main keel, where the freight and mail rooms, fuel, water, supplies and spare parts were also located, a typical crewman stood watches of four hours on duty and eight hours off. The day-to-day navigation and control of the ship were the responsibility of the officer of the watch; the captain, who had a sleeping cabin in the keel just forward of the control car, did not stand watch, but he was on call at all times.

One of the most exacting tasks was that of the elevator man, whose job was to maintain correct altitude and keep the ship flying on a level plane. Standing sideways, his feet planted firmly fore and aft, a skilled elevator man could feel whether his ship was nosing up or down, and operate his control wheel accordingly. (The work was so exhausting that elevator men stood watches of just two or three hours, instead of four.) It took years of experience to make a good elevator man, and each one had his own style—a veteran officer in his cabin could tell which man was at the elevator wheel from the way he handled the ship in gusty weather. The elevator men on the *Hindenburg* were especially skilled. They always tried not to allow the ship to go up or down more than 5 degrees by the nose—above that angle the wine bottles fell over on the dining tables—but the slant was rarely more than 2 degrees, an angle barely noticeable even at mealtime.

Transatlantic passengers' fares during the *Hindenburg's* first year were $400 one way and $720 round trip—compared with $273 and $519 on the liners *Normandie* and *Queen Mary*—and as winter closed the 1936 season it was proposed that these rates be raised to $450 and $810 in 1937. On both the North America and South America runs, commercial Zeppelin operations were at last turning a modest profit; it seemed that airship travel was an idea whose time had come. Two new Zeppelins were scheduled to join the *Hindenburg*. One, designated the LZ 130, would have space for 100 passengers; the other, LZ 131, was designed to accommodate 150.

So bright did prospects seem that in the winter of 1936-1937 a new international company—the American Zeppelin Transport Corporation—was formed. In cooperation with the Zeppelin Reederei it was to build and operate two additional airship liners. Eckener hoped that airship flights would be extended eastward to the Dutch East Indies and then, perhaps, across the Pacific. Because weather conditions at Lakehurst often were not ideal for airship handling, he had already scouted the proposed site of a big new American airship port at Alexandria, Virginia, on the Potomac River just south of Washington, D.C. Meanwhile, because the hydrogen-filled *Hindenburg* now had greater disposable lift than it would if inflated with heavier helium as originally planned, nine additional passenger cabins were built on B deck.

At the start of the 1937 season, the Zeppelin Reederei was thus

Its unprecedented girth emphasized in this view, the Hindenburg prepares for a landing at Frankfurt by releasing water ballast to slow its descent.

poised for a breakthrough in commercial airship operations. The *Graf Zeppelin* was scheduled for 20 more flights to South America; the *Hindenburg* was scheduled for 18 round trips to the United States. And the new LZ 130 was scheduled to make its first flight to Rio on October 27. In all, at least 78 Atlantic crossings by Zeppelin were planned for 1937.

The *Hindenburg's* first 1937 flight to Lakehurst was due to originate from the new Rhein-Main World Airport on the evening of May 3. The flying season seemed to be getting off to a slow start, for only 36 passengers were booked to make the flight, and some of these were traveling on complimentary passes as guests of the Reederei. Nor had a great deal of cargo been checked on board—apart from bags of mail there were news films, tobacco leaf samples, fancy goods, airplane parts, a lady's dress, two dogs and three fertile partridge eggs. On the other hand there was an unusually large complement of 61 officers and men, 20 of whom were undergoing flight training before being assigned to the LZ 130 and LZ 131.

In command of the flight was Max Pruss, a veteran of World War I airship service and a former captain of the *Graf Zeppelin.* With him for the season's inaugural were four other experienced captains, including Ernst Lehmann, the operational chief of Zeppelin Reederei.

Lehmann's last-minute decision to make the trip may well have been prompted by a letter received by the German Ambassador in Washington, warning that the *Hindenburg* might be a target of sabotage. The Ambassador had received many such letters and phone calls from anti-Nazis in the United States, but this one seemed different, and he had passed it on to Lehmann. Written by one Kathie Rauch of Milwaukee, Wisconsin, the letter urged the Ambassador to "inform the Zeppelin Company in Frankfurt-am-Main that they should open and search all mail before it is put on board prior to *every* flight of the Zeppelin *Hindenburg.* The Zeppelin is going to be destroyed by a time bomb during its flight to another country. Please believe my words as the truth, so that no one later will have cause for regret."

At 7 p.m. on May 3, the ship's passengers were picked up at their luxury hotel, the Frankfurter Hof, and bused to the airport. The *Hindenburg* had already been walked out of its hangar; it stood motionless and majestic, tethered by its nose cone to a short mast and illuminated by searchlights that gave it an otherworldly appearance. German security officers had searched the ship and the passengers' baggage for sabotage devices; now the airline checked the passengers for anything that might cause a spark—matches, lighters, even flashlights—before finally allowing them to mount the narrow gangway and board the ship.

At 8:15 p.m. the *Hindenburg* was detached from the mast and floated slowly and silently into the air as a brass band in blue-and-yellow uniforms began beating out the German national anthem and the Nazi rallying song, "Horst Wessel Lied." To one passenger, the curiously ethereal ascension was like "a lift and pull upward, an indescribable

Passengers on the Hindenburg's promenade deck wave to friends on the ground from canted windows that were often left open, as there was no draft even at cruising speed. The lower rank of windows was built into the floor of B deck.

feeling of lightness and buoyancy." At 300 feet Pruss signaled "half ahead" and the music from the ground was drowned by the deep-throated bass roar of the engines. The ship headed northward through the night at a cruising speed of almost 90 miles per hour.

After flying over the Netherlands and down the English Channel, the *Hindenburg* turned out over the Atlantic and passed the south coast of Ireland. A strong head wind cut its ground speed to a slow 60 miles per hour, threatening to make the crossing an unusually tedious one. True, the standards of comfort were as superb as ever. The food was outstanding and even in stormy weather the ship was smooth and steady. But there was an uncharacteristic listlessness among the passengers, and one of them complained to his wife that it was the most uneventful journey he had ever undertaken in an airship. The usually cordial Ernst Lehmann, who was mourning the recent death of his young son, was plunged in gloom and was late for meals. All through Tuesday, the

Passengers gaze from windows tilted outward on the Hindenburg's promenade deck. At night, curtains kept the ship's interior lights from interfering with the view.

As he would in a fine hotel, a passenger leaves his shoes outside his stateroom for shining by a steward during the night.

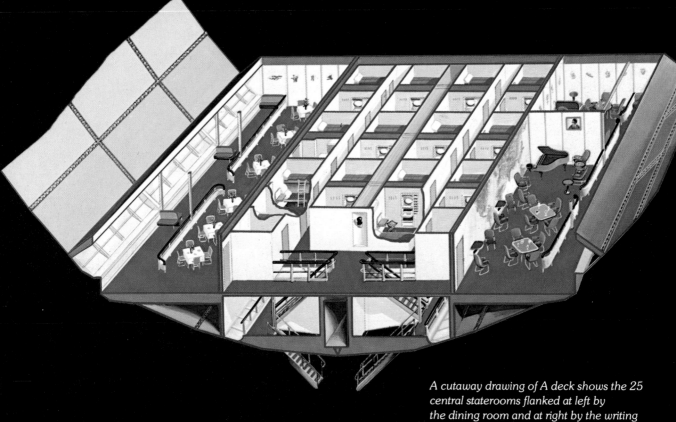

A cutaway drawing of A deck shows the 25 central staterooms flanked at left by the dining room and at right by the writing room (rear) and the lounge.

New levels of spacious splendor

The *Hindenburg's* accommodations redefined the already high standards of airship-passenger comfort. Where the smaller *Graf Zeppelin* had a single public room, 16½ feet square (smoking forbidden), the double-decked *Hindenburg* offered a dining room 50 feet long, a 34-foot lounge, a writing room, a bar and a hydrogenproof smoking room.

The sleeping cabins on the *Hindenburg* lacked the *Graf's* windows but did offer hot and cold running water and heated air. These features, augmented by the stewards' attentive service, justified Hugo Eckener's claim that a voyage in the lap of *Hindenburg* luxury was an experience of "incomparable charm."

The Hindenburg's 34-place dining room is filled to capacity for a sumptuous meal that might include venison or roast gosling.

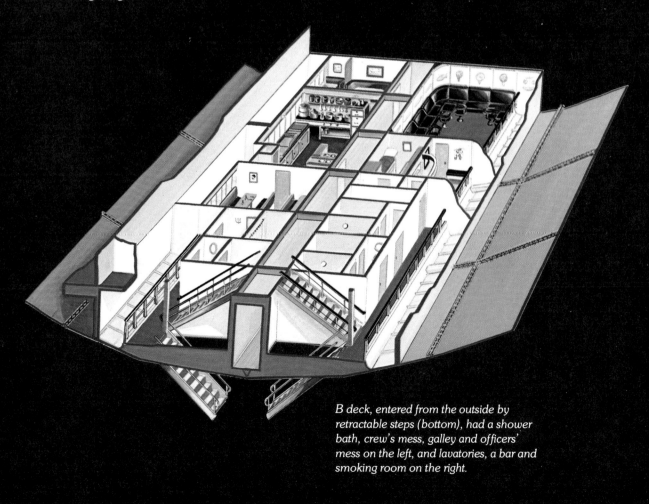

B deck, entered from the outside by retractable steps (bottom), had a shower bath, crew's mess, galley and officers' mess on the left, and lavatories, a bar and smoking room on the right.

second day out, the great ship butted the persistent Atlantic winds, and even Captain Pruss admitted to a passenger that this was shaping up as "one of the worst trips" he had ever made.

It was now inevitable that the arrival in America would be behind schedule. At 6 a.m. on Wednesday, May 5, the *Hindenburg* was still flying into a 50-mile head wind east of St. John's, Newfoundland, and the weather on the North American coast was deteriorating. All day the ship fought its way westward as severe electrical storms began to develop ahead. The *Hindenburg* was due in at Lakehurst at 6 a.m. on Thursday, May 6, but at dawn on that day it was still flying low over coastal waters off New England. As the morning wore on, the winds reduced the ship's speed to a plodding 37 miles per hour, and its arrival was reset for 6 p.m., a full 12 hours late. At 11:36 a.m. the ship came down very low to give the passengers a look at Boston. At 3:07 it passed the skyscrapers of Manhattan, flying over the Empire State Building and a National League baseball game between the Brooklyn Dodgers and the Pittsburgh Pirates at Ebbets Field.

Just before 4 p.m. Lakehurst advised by radio that there was considerable turbulence in the area, with gusts up to 30 miles per hour. A few minutes later Pruss brought the *Hindenburg* over the base, but ominous-looking black clouds, heavy rain squalls and swirling winds kept him from attempting a landing. Pruss wrote a message—"Riding out the storm"—and dropped it over the side with a small weight attached. Then he cruised slowly southward to the mouth of the Delaware River and waited for word of improved conditions at Lakehurst.

At 5:43 p.m. Commander Charles Rosendahl, now the commanding officer of the Naval Air Station at Lakehurst, advised a further delay. Forty minutes later the cloud ceiling had risen, the wind had dropped and the thunderstorms had practically cleared. Rosendahl, anxious for the *Hindenburg* to get in quickly while the opportunity existed, radioed again: RECOMMEND LANDING NOW. But Pruss, a cautious operator, still stood off. Rosendahl's next message, at 7:10, was more urgent: CONDITIONS DEFINITELY IMPROVED. RECOMMEND EARLIEST POSSIBLE LANDING.

This time Pruss responded, and the *Hindenburg* came in through the last rain curtain as lightning still flickered on the stormy horizon. When the airship hangar at Lakehurst came into view, Pruss ordered his crew to their landing stations. The stewards had finished piling up bed linen in the ship's corridors and Lehmann was saying quick good-bys to the passengers before taking up a post in the control car. Those who had finished their packing and paid their wine bills began to line up in the main lounge in readiness for passport inspection.

The *Hindenburg* came in for a prelanding check fast and low—84 miles per hour at 590 feet. A large crowd of spectators had gathered to watch it come in; in addition to the families and friends of the passengers, and the 138 civilian and 92 Navy ground handlers, a number of reporters, cameramen, professional and amateur photographers were waiting to record the arrival. Despite the demise of the United States

Navy's airship program, the American public remained enthusiastic about the comings and goings of the German Zeppelins.

One of the reporters was Herb Morrison, of the Chicago radio station WLS, who began to record his commentary as the *Hindenburg* roared up through the gathering dusk:

"Here it comes, ladies and gentlemen, and what a sight it is, a thrilling one, a marvelous sight. It is coming down out of the sky pointed toward us, and toward the mooring mast. The mighty diesel motors roar, the propellers biting into the air. No one wonders that this great floating palace can travel through the air at such a speed with these powerful motors behind it."

Pruss slowed the engines to "idle ahead" and took the *Hindenburg* on a cautious circuit of the field. At 7:20 p.m. he brought the ship in level for landing with the engines set at "idle astern." At reduced speed and at an altitude of 200 feet, the ship was pointed into the wind, bearing for the landing party below. As it nudged toward the mooring mast, the wind suddenly shifted and Pruss made a quick, tight turn to get its nose back into the wind. At 7:21, with the ship still at 200 feet and at a distance of about 700 feet from the mast, crewmen dropped the forward handling lines out of the nose of the ship; the lines were seized by members of the ground party and connected to the main mooring lines.

For Commander Rosendahl, the landing was proceeding routinely, though the huge Zeppelin was still an awesome sight. "There in imposing, majestic silence," he recalled afterward, "the vast silvery bulk of the *Hindenburg* hung motionless like a framed, populated cloud. Everything within and without the ship was proceeding in an entirely normal manner. In only a few minutes more the ship would reach the ground and her mooring mast safely and smoothly."

Passengers peered down from the promenade windows and waved to friends on the ground; customs inspectors and other officials were making their way toward the mooring mast to clear the passengers for entry to the United States. The ship was now at 75 feet and stationary. Everything was in good order on board and nothing untoward was noticed on the control-room instruments. It was 7:25 p.m.

Inside the ship's huge lower tail fin, four crewmen stood by to drop the stern lines. Two of them happened to be looking in the direction of the No. 4 after gas cell, some 50 feet ahead and above them, when a sudden bright flash of red, blue and yellow fire—initially no more than three feet in diameter—appeared in the center of the cell. It was accompanied by a low popping sound like a gas burner being lighted on a stove. Then the entire cell blew up with a muffled detonation and the men in the tail found themselves surrounded by fire.

At the same moment an eyewitness on the ground noticed "a faint pink glow" in the lower center of the ship. Another saw the stern light up "sort of like a Japanese lantern," and watched the flames inside swirl and illuminate the outer cover so that the silhouette of the framework was visible through the fabric. Commander Rosendahl saw a small burst of flame just forward of the upper vertical fin; the orange ball swelled almost instantaneously into a towering mushroom shape as brilliant as "a million magnesium flares" and lighted up the great airship's interior.

The passengers were not immediately aware of the disaster that was overwhelming their vessel. Some were still packing their bags in their remote inside cabins, others stood with their baggage at the big windows along the promenade decks. Their first hint that something was wrong came when they saw the people on the ground suddenly stiffen, then turn and run from the ship as a faint rosy glow reflected over the wet, sandy ground. Seconds later the passenger decks were on fire. Long, bright, red flames lapped through the cabins and public rooms, and people and furniture slid in chaos as the ship sank steeply by the stern. Passengers rushed and screamed among the flames; one man hurled himself against a window rail and cried: "It is the end!"

The officers and men in the control room, situated forward and directly underneath the burning hull, were among the last to learn of the fire. The shock of the initial detonation had reached them only faintly and momentarily perplexed them.

"Is a rope broken?" one of the officers asked Pruss.

"No," Pruss replied. "What is it?"

All the officers looked at one another questioningly. Then they heard the chief radio officer, Willy Speck, shouting from the radio room above the control car: "The ship's burning!" Through the control-car windows the air glowed with a strange yellow color. One officer instinctively ran about looking for the ship's logbook as the rudderman began to moan, "Oh, oh, oh, oh. . . ." Pruss made a split-second decision not to drop water ballast—the standard procedure to prevent a ship's fall—but to let the stern sink to the ground so that at least the people in that part of the ship would have a chance of getting out alive. But as the stern fell the bow rose until it was pointing high in the air several hundred feet above the ground. At this steep angle, 11 of the 12 men stationed in the nose cone lost their grip and plunged backward into the rapidly advancing fire. Passengers who were preparing to leap from the windows pulled back as the ground receded from them, seeing that to jump would mean instant death—though some lost their footing and plummeted to earth anyway, legs thrashing.

Suddenly a 100-foot tongue of fire shot out of the nose like a flame from a monstrous blowtorch, and the ship, now ablaze from end to end, began to fall. One survivor described the situation on board as "a scene from a medieval picture of hell." Burning fabric and melting duralumin rained down on the struggling passengers and crew; the ground handlers fled in terror as the *Hindenburg's* fiery carcass descended toward them with a deep hissing sound. It crashed only 20 feet from some of them, flattening slightly as its white-hot structure collapsed and spilled human figures that came leaping and stumbling through the flames. "Navy men, stand fast!" cried their leader, Chief Boatswain Fred "Bull" Tobin, as the airship hit. "We've got to get those people out of there!"

The ground crew at the Naval Air Station at Lakehurst, New Jersey, strains at the Hindenburg's spider lines. While hovering to land, the buoyant ship was difficult to control in even a light breeze, and had to be hauled down manually for mooring.

Bracing their poles, called crutches, against rails on the control car, Navy crewmen help position the Hindenburg for mooring to a mobile mast at Lakehurst. Low-pressure tires on shock-absorbing mountings protected the control car and lower fin from contact with the ground.

The Navy men—and some civilians too—turned and, according to one eyewitness, "dived into the flames like dogs after rabbits."

Only 32 seconds had passed from the moment the first flame appeared in the stern to the time the *Hindenburg's* bow hit the ground. It did not seem possible that anyone could have lived through such a holocaust, but survivors continued to pour from the flaming wreck. Their survival was a matter of chance. The men in the tail who had first seen the fire start walked out virtually unhurt because the flames and heat had gone upward, sparing those in the lower fin. One passenger found himself on the ground surrounded by burning wreckage and burrowed his way out through the wet sand. Another passenger, a professional acrobat, was able to hang from a window sill all the time the ship was falling, dropping off only when he was a safe height from the ground. A cabin boy survived the heat when a water tank emptied its contents over him. One mother tossed her children out of a window and they survived. An elderly woman, dazed by the catastrophe, simply walked down the ship's gangway in the normal way. Many survivors had no clear idea how they got out—one simply found himself crawling on his hands and knees across the sand.

The 12 officers and men in the control car were the last to leave. As the car wheel hit the ground Pruss gave his last order of the flight: "Now! Everybody out!" Lehmann then leaped through a small window forward on the starboard side and, with Captain Pruss and another officer, attempted to escape as glowing girderwork began to crash down around them. Pruss turned back to rescue Willy Speck, who was trapped, mortally injured, in the wreckage; he was badly burned about the face as he did so. Lehmann came out with his clothes on fire and his back seared from his head to the base of his spine as if by a welder's torch. "I don't understand it," he mumbled as he was led away in shock. The *Hindenburg's* remaining senior officer, Captain Anton Wittemann, waited by the control car until a gap presented itself on the upwind port side and he was able to walk out unscathed. Another officer remained close to the burning car and covered his head, feet and hands with wet sand; when the fire burned down he walked to safety.

By 7:26 on the evening of May 6, 1937, the *Hindenburg,* the finest airship and the largest and most luxurious aircraft ever built, lay a smoldering, smoke-blackened skeleton on the sodden soil of New Jersey. Miraculously, 62 people had survived the holocaust and only 36 had lost their lives, including one ground crew member and 13 fare-paying passengers. Among the survivors was Max Pruss, the ship's last captain. Among those who would not survive was Ernst Lehmann. The man who had bombed London in LZ 98, flown sorties on the Eastern Front, helped fly the *Graf Zeppelin* around the world and piloted the first scheduled intercontinental flights in history died of second- and third-degree burns 24 hours after the disaster.

Word of the catastrophe traveled quickly overseas. Hugo Eckener got the news when a Berlin-based *New York Times* correspondent

Passengers on the Hindenburg descend one of its gangways at Lakehurst after an Atlantic crossing in 1936. Bicycle-like wheels on a mobile landing stair allowed it to be repositioned as the wind moved the airship slowly at its mooring mast.

roused him with a telephone call about 2 a.m. German time, less than an hour after the blazing Zeppelin had crumpled to the ground. "Dr. Eckener," explained the voice on the phone, "I felt it was necessary to inform you. . . ." Aghast, the 68-year-old airship pioneer made immediate plans to travel to Lakehurst by sea with Ludwig Dürr and other experts to investigate the crash. Meanwhile Captain Hans von Schiller, commanding the *Graf Zeppelin* on a scheduled flight from Rio, received the news by radio while cruising over the Atlantic near the Canary Islands. At first he dismissed it as a journalistic hoax. Then he received a second message: REGRET HINDENBURG REPORT CONFIRMED. The stunned Schiller resolved not to tell his passengers until the *Graf* was safely landed; he pressed on for home on what was to be the last rigid-airship passenger flight in history.

Eckener reached the scene of the disaster eight days later. *"Traurig,"* he muttered in sorrow as he looked at the twisted carcass of his most magnificent ship. "Sad." Then the tough, gruff old man silently wept. "It appeared to me the hopeless end of a great dream," he was to write later, "a kind of end of the world."

What had caused the *Hindenburg* to catch fire? Explanations were plentiful, but they boiled down in the end to two principal theories: sabotage or the ignition of a hydrogen leak by some natural source of electricity. But the fire had obliterated almost all clues, and separate German and American inquiries found little evidence to explain the explosion. The sabotage theory—an incendiary bullet fired from outside the ship or a time bomb placed inside it—was shared by Rosendahl and several of the *Hindenburg's* officers and men, including Max Pruss and Ernst Lehmann, who as he lay dying told Rosendahl: "It must have been an infernal machine." The finger of suspicion was pointed variously at one of the crew members and at one of the passengers, without a shred of solid evidence. The ominous letter that had led Lehmann to take the fatal flight was a blind alley: Kathie Rauch had merely communicated the forebodings of an eccentric dabbler in the occult who told her that he had dreamed of seeing the *Hindenburg* in flames.

In the end, both the American and German investigating commissions concluded that a mixture of hydrogen and air in the vicinity of gas cells 4 and 5 probably had been ignited by an electrical charge—either a static spark or St. Elmo's fire, a discharge of electricity that sometimes occurs on the prominent parts of ships and aircraft in stormy weather. There was no proof either way at the time, but in later years two reliable witnesses were found who claimed they had seen a blue flame of St. Elmo's fire flicker along the backbone girder of the *Hindenburg* a minute before the ship caught fire.

The widely publicized destruction of the *Hindenburg* did not mark the immediate end of the rigid airship. The LZ 130, a ship of similar dimensions to the *Hindenburg,* was nearly completed; construction of the LZ 131, an eight-million-cubic-foot super *Hindenburg,* was about to begin. The recently formed American Zeppelin Transport Corporation still planned to operate an expanded schedule of transatlantic service with two ships, in close cooperation with the Reederei, and Eckener hoped that public confidence in airship travel could be restored. But he knew that the commercial Zeppelin was finished unless he could obtain helium from America; after the *Hindenburg* disaster, no passenger flights with hydrogen-inflated ships could ever be permitted again.

For the aging *Graf Zeppelin,* no reprieve was possible. The most successful airship of them all, the *Graf* had flown 1,060,000 miles (becoming the first aircraft in history to fly more than a million miles), had crossed the Atlantic 144 times and had carried more than 13,000 passengers in its nine-year career. But the ship would not have enough lift for transoceanic flying if it was inflated with helium, and in June 1937 it was ferried to Frankfurt, deflated and put on public display.

For a time it seemed likely that Eckener might succeed. The Americans' shock at the burning of the *Hindenburg,* coupled with discoveries of huge new deposits of helium gas, persuaded the United States government to agree to export a limited quantity of helium to Germany

The Hindenburg displays its swastikas over Berlin's flag-draped Brandenburg Gate during the 1936 Olympics. Nazi leaders had little use for the dirigibles, except as vehicles for propaganda.

under strict control. Then in March 1938, Hitler moved into Austria and rekindled fears of a European war. Harold Ickes, the Secretary of the Interior and chairman of the Helium Commission, promptly refused to release any of the vital gas to Germany, fearing that a helium-inflated Zeppelin could still serve a military purpose.

Ickes was right enough. In September 1938—the centenary year of Count Ferdinand von Zeppelin's birth—the LZ 130 was christened *Graf Zeppelin II* and launched on its maiden flight under the command of 70-year-old Eckener himself. The hydrogen-filled ship was then taken over by the German Air Force, the Luftwaffe. Electronic surveillance equipment was set up in its passenger accommodations, and under the command of Captain Albert Sammt, a *Hindenburg* survivor, the ship was flown on at least nine missions along the borders of Czechoslovakia, Poland, the Netherlands and Great Britain, in order to observe the electronic and radar defenses of those nations. On a two-day spy flight along the east coast of Britain at the end of May 1939, and another 48-hour flight to Scotland in early August, the LZ 130 almost changed the course of the War that finally came only a few weeks later. The flights were intended to probe Britain's still-secret early-warning electronic defense system, but with their receptors tuned to the wrong wavelength, the Germans failed to detect the British radar, which went on to play a crucial role in blunting the Luftwaffe's edge during the Battle of Britain.

The Zeppelin had no place in that battle, though the United States Navy later put a fleet of more than 150 nonrigid blimps into the air. Deployed in 15 airship squadrons, these blimps were used primarily as convoy escorts and on antisubmarine patrols over Atlantic, Pacific and Mediterranean waters. Not one vessel sailing under a blimp escort was ever sunk by an enemy submarine, and only a single blimp, brought down by gunfire from a surfaced U-boat, was lost to enemy action. But large rigid airships were absent from the skies during the whole of World War II. Indeed, in early 1940, Luftwaffe chief Hermann Göring ordered the destruction of the only two existing Zeppelins on the ground that their metal was needed for the construction of military aircraft. Pleas that the old *Graf Zeppelin* be preserved were ignored. The ship was pulled to bits and its parts sent to the Netherlands to make a German radar tower.

The two great hangars at Frankfurt were blown up with the explanation that they hindered the takeoffs of Luftwaffe bombers. Most of the Zeppelin officers and crewmen were dispersed into war service. The *Hindenburg's* last captain, Max Pruss, became commandant of Frankfurt's airport—by then a Luftwaffe base. The *Graf Zeppelin's* last captain, Hans von Schiller, headed the port of Cologne. Hugo Eckener continued in harness as nominal chairman of the Zeppelin Company, which survived by making armaments.

By 1944 the Zeppelin construction sheds at Friedrichshafen had been flattened by British and American bombers, and after the War virtually nothing tangible was left of the Zeppelin works. As for the Zeppelin dream, it was but a faint memory of a bygone day.

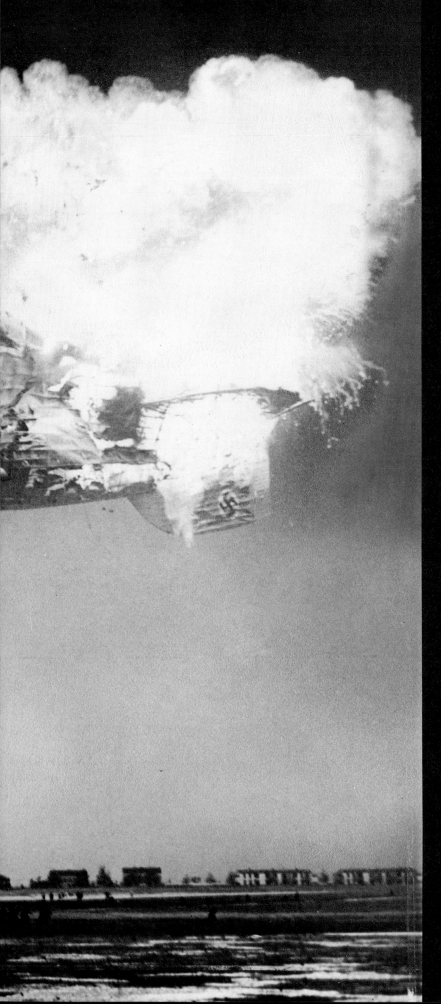

The noble dream consumed in flame

The arrival of the *Hindenburg,* a little behind schedule, at Lakehurst, New Jersey, on the evening of May 6, 1937, promised to be routine. The ship had an unblemished safety record on 18 previous Atlantic crossings. In fact, no passenger had ever lost his life on any commercial airship. Still, because this was the beginning of the most ambitious season yet planned for airship voyages, reporters, photographers and newsreel cameramen had their eyes and lenses focused on the great dirigible as it approached.

When disaster struck it was sudden. Without warning, flames gushed from within the *Hindenburg's* hull; 32 seconds later the airship lay on the ground, ravaged. Never had the sights and sounds of a disaster in progress been so graphically documented, or so swiftly disseminated. Within a day, newspaper readers and theater audiences were confronted by the fiery images shown on these pages. Radio listeners heard the emotional words of newsman Herb Morrison, sobbing into his recorder: "It's burning, bursting into flames, and it's falling on the mooring mast and all the folks. This is one of the worst catastrophes in the world. . . . Oh, the humanity and all the passengers!"

Thus amplified, the demise of the *Hindenburg* had a searing impact on public consciousness that far transcended the bare statistics of the calamity. The final count was 35 dead, including 13 passengers. Nearly two thirds of the 97 persons on board survived, but that fact was forever obscured, and the name *Hindenburg* became a synonym for human-wrought tragedy comparable only to the name *Titanic.*

The burning of the *Hindenburg* made it clear once and for all that dirigible travel was merely a blind alley in the evolution of flight. The giant airships' remaining loyalists were left to muse, along with Gill Robb Wilson, the landing supervisor at Lakehurst that fateful evening: "Those of us long in the air know what it is to reach out in salute to the embodiment of our hopes, and suddenly find our fingers filled with ashes."

Above the field at Lakehurst, fully half the Hindenburg is in flames scant seconds after ignition, and crewmen on the ground begin to run for their lives.

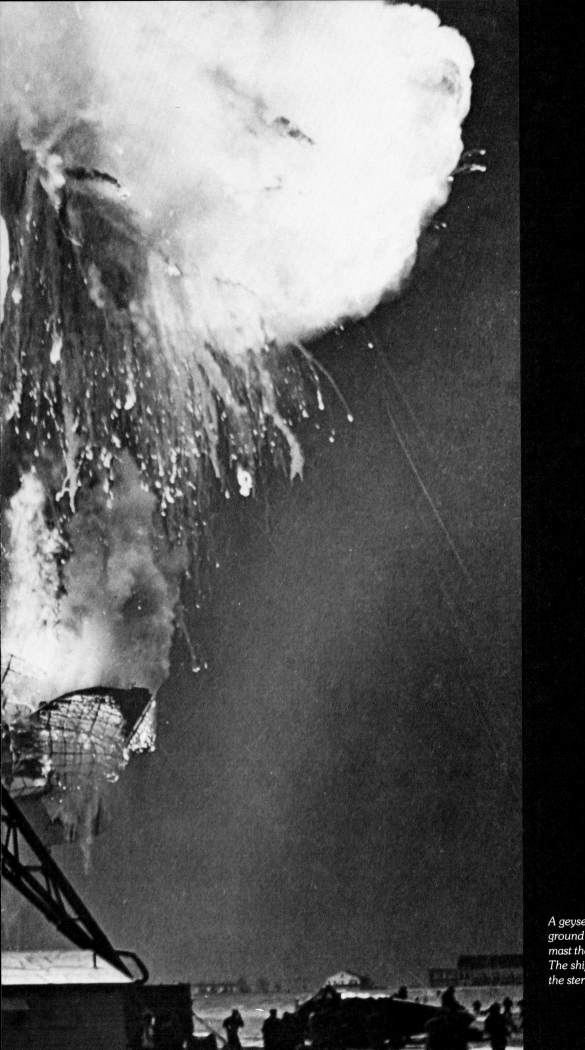

A geyser of burning hydrogen silhouettes ground crewmen stationed on the mooring mast the Hindenburg never reached. The ship's bow, still intact, rises sharply as the stern dissolves in flame.

Flames shoot out from the nose of the
Hindenburg as the hull settles over the
grounded passenger section. The airship's
stern has already been totally consumed.

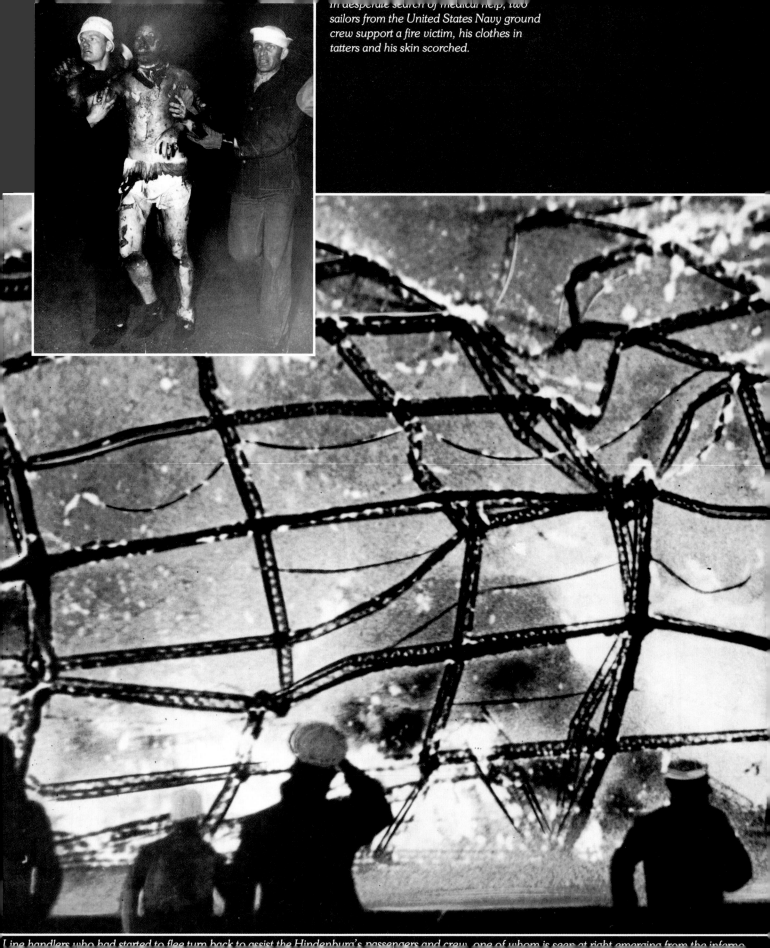

In desperate search of medical help, two sailors from the United States Navy ground crew support a fire victim, his clothes in tatters and his skin scorched.

Line handlers who had started to flee turn back to assist the Hindenburg's passengers and crew, one of whom is seen at right emerging from the inferno.

A frantic civilian at right daubs the burns of a passenger whose face is a mask of shock and disbelief. He was among the 62 who survived the ordeal.

Their arms linked, four dazed but relatively unscathed Hindenburg survivors, including the first officer, Albert Sammt, support one another as they stumble to safety.

While smoke billows from the Hindenburg's still-burning diesel fuel, clusters of the curious gather to view the charred remains of the airship—and the airship dream.

Acknowledgments

The index for this book was prepared by Gale Linck Partoyan. For their help in the preparation of this book, the editors wish to thank Frank Wootton, artist *(endpaper and cover detail, regular edition),* Frederic F. Bigio, artist *(pages 23 and 60),* John Batchelor, artist *(pages 104-107 and 156-157),* Lloyd K. Townsend, artist *(pages 106-107)* and Walter Roberts, cartographer *(pages 92-93).*

For their valuable help with the preparation of this volume, the editors wish to thank: **In France:** Paris—Henriette Angel; Gérard Baschet, Éditions de l'*Illustration;* André Bénard, Odile Benoist, Elisabeth Caquot, Alain Degardin, Georges Delaleau, Gilbert Deloizy, Général Paul Dompnier, Deputy Director, Yvan Kayser, Général Pierre Lissarague, Director, Stephane Nicolaou, Colonel Jean-Baptiste Reveilhac, Curator, Musée de l'Air; Edmond Petit, Curator, Musée Air-France; Jean Robert, Curator, Musée National des Techniques. **In Great Britain:** Cardington—Frank Kiernan, Mrs. M. Neaderson, Royal Aircraft Establishment; Farnborough— Robert S. Lawrie, Brian C. Kervell, Alec Stenbridge, Royal Aircraft Establishment; London—Lindsay Fulcher, Museum of London; J. S. Lucas, M. J. Willis, J. O. Simmonds, Imperial War Museum; R. W. Mack, Royal Air Force Museum; John Maggs; Arnold Nayler, Michael Fitzgerald, Royal Aeronautical Society; John Bagley, Martin Andrewartha, National Aeronautical Collection, Wendy Sheridan, Pictorial Collection, Science Museum; Marjorie Willis, BBC Hulton Picture Library. **In Italy:** Bracciano—General Giuseppe Pesce, Director, Museo Storico Dell'Aeronautica Militare, Vigna di Valle; Milan—Maurizio Pagliano; Rome— Colonel Gennaro Adamo, Stato Maggiore Aeronautica; Contessa Maria Fede Caproni, Museo Aeronautico di Taliedo; Dr. Gertrude Nobile. **In Japan:** Tokyo—Tadashi Nazawa. **In the United States:** California—Tom Kassis, Nut Tree Associates; Martha H. Kennedy, California Historical Society; David Kuhner, Carruthers History of Aviation Collection, Claremont Colleges; Gary F. Kurutz, California State Library; Lee Payne; Patricia Rieffanaugh, Leach Corporation Heritage of the Air Collection; Colorado—Donald J. Barrett, Air Force Academy Library; Washington, D.C.—Edwin J. Kirschner, American Airship Association; Donald W. Mansfield; J. Gordon Vaeth; Edgar A. Wischnowski; Illinois—Cheryl Johnson; Dennis Kromm; John T. McCutcheon Jr., *Chicago Tribune;* Roy D. Schickedanz; New Jersey—Nick Grand, U.S. Navy Air Engineering Center; New York City—Frank Braynard; Joan Michaelis, Goodyear; Lawrence Miller; Ohio—Gary Arnold, Ohio Historical Society; Marjory Garman, Thomas B. Riley, Goodyear Tire & Rubber Company; Kathy Louie, Western Reserve Historical Society; John V. Miller, University of Akron; Arlene J. Peterson, Ohio Historical Center; Lyle Schwilling, Goodyear Aerospace Corporation; Texas—Marvin A. Krieger; Mr. and Mrs. G. Edward Rice, George H. Williams Jr., History of Aviation Collection, The University of Texas at Dallas; Charles M. Robinson III. **In West Germany:** Broistedt—Peter Amesbury; Cuxhaven—Gerhard Hibscher, Kapitänleutnant; Erdweg: Hans-Georg Knäusel; Friedrichshafen— Ernst Fischbach; Willy Kaldenbach, Director, Manfred A. Sauter, Luftschiffbau Zeppelin, GmbH.; Zeppelin Museum der Stadt Friedrichshafen; Hamburg—Dr. Karl Clausberg; Kurt Puzicha, Marine-Luftschiffer-Kameradschaft; Koblenz—Meinrad Nilges, Bundesarchiv Koblenz; Lübeck—Werner Vermehren, Kapitänleutnant; Mittelbiberach—Ursula Gräfin Brandenstein-Zeppelin; Neu-Isenburg—Oskar Fink, Zeppelinheim; Nordholz—Captain Claus-Peter Brandt, Marinefliegergeschwader 3 "Graf Zeppelin"; Schlüchtern—Isa Gräfin Brandenstein-Zeppelin; West Berlin—Dr. Roland Klemig, Heidi Klein, Bildarchiv Preussischer Kulturbesitz; Axel Schulz, Ullstein Bilderdienst. The editors also wish to thank JoAnne Reid, Chicago; Rose-Mary Hall Cason, Dallas; Mary Castanheira, Lisbon.

Particularly useful sources of information and quotations used in this volume were *Who Destroyed the Hindenburg?* by A. A. Hoehling, Little, Brown, 1962; *The Millionth Chance: The Story of the R. 101,* by James Leasor, Reynal and Company, 1957; *Giants in the Sky: A History of the Rigid Airship* by Douglas H. Robinson, University of Washington Press, 1973; *The Zeppelin in Combat: A History of the German Naval Airship Division, 1912-1918* by Douglas H. Robinson, G. T. Foulis & Co Ltd, 1971; and *Santos-Dumont: A Study in Obsession* by Peter Wykeham, Harcourt, Brace & World, Inc., 1962.

Bibliography

Abbott, Patrick, *Airship: The Story of R 34 and the First East-West Crossing of the Atlantic by Air.* Charles Scribner's Sons, 1973.

American Heritage, *History of Flight.* American Heritage Publishing Co., Inc., 1962.

Amundsen, Roald, and Lincoln Ellsworth, *First Crossing of the Polar Sea.* George H. Doran Company, 1927.

Beaubois, Henry, *Airships Yesterday, Today and Tomorrow.* The Two Continents Publishing Group Ltd., 1976.

Brooks, Peter W., *Historic Airships.* New York Graphic Society Ltd., 1973.

Buttlar Brandenfels, Treusch von, *Zeppelins over England.* London: George G. Harrap & Co. Ltd.

Charlton, L. E. O., *War over England.* London: Longmans, Green and Co., 1936.

Clarke, Basil, *Polar Flight.* London: Ian Allan, 1964.

Clausberg, Karl, *Zeppelin: Die Geschichte eines unwahrscheinlichen Erfolges.* Munich: Schirmer/Mosel, 1979.

Collier, Basil, *The Airship: A History.* G. P. Putnam's Sons, 1974.

Cross, Wilbur, *Ghost Ship of the Pole.* William Sloane Associates, 1960.

Davy, M. J. B., *Handbook of the Collections Illustrating Aeronautics—II: Lighter-than-air Craft.* London: His Majesty's Stationery Office, 1934.

Deighton, Len, and Arnold Schwartzman, *Airshipwreck.* Holt, Rinehart and Winston, 1978.

Dieckerhoff, Otto, *Deutsche Luftschiffe 1914-1918.* 1973.

Dollfus, Charles, and Henri Bouché, *Histoire de L'Aéronautique.* Paris: L'Illustration, 1942.

Eckener, Hugo, *My Zeppelins.* London: Putnam, 1958.

Ege, Lennart, *Balloons and Airships.* Macmillan Publishing Co., Inc., 1974.

Geisenheyner, Max, *Mit "Graf Zeppelin" um die Welt: Ein Bild-Buch.* 1929.

Gibbs-Smith, Charles Harvard, *Aviation: An Historical Survey from Its Origins to the End of World War II.* London: Her Majesty's Stationery Office, 1970.

Glines, C. V., *Polar Aviation.* Franklin Watts, Inc., 1964.

Goebel, J., *40000 km Zeppelin-Kriegsfahrten: Lettow-Vorbeck entgegen.* Leipzig: Verlag von K. F. Koehler, 1931.

Haining, Peter, *The Dream Machines.* London: New English Library, 1972.

Hallam, T. D., *The Spider Web: The Romance of a Flying-Boat Flight in the First World War.* London: Arms and Armour Press, 1979.

Hartcup, Guy, *The Achievement of the Airship: A History of the Development of Rigid, Semi-rigid and Non-rigid Airships.* David & Charles Inc., 1974.

Hearne, R. P., *Zeppelins and Super-Zeppelins.* London: John Lane, 1916.

Heiss, *Das Zeppelinbuch.* Berlin: Volk und Reich Verlag, 1936.

Higham, Robin, *The British Rigid Airship, 1908-1931: A Study in Weapons Policy.* Greenwood Press, 1975.

Hildebrandt, A., *Balloons and Airships.* Yorkshire: EP Publishing Limited, 1973.

Hildebrandt, Hans, *Zeppelin-Denkmal für das Deutsche Volk.* Stuttgart: Germania-Verlag GmbH.

Hoehling, A. A., *Who Destroyed the Hindenburg?* Little, Brown, 1962.

Hook, Thom:
Shenandoah Saga. Air Show Publishers, 1973.
Sky Ship: The Akron Era. Airshow Publishers, 1976.

Horton, Edward, *The Age of the Airship.* Henry Regnery Company, 1973.

Hoyt, Edwin P., *The Zeppelins.* Lothrop, Lee & Shepard Co., 1969.

Italiaander, Rolf, *Hugo Eckener Ein moderner Columbus: Die Weltgeltung der Zeppelin-Luftschiffahrt in Bildern und Dokumenten.* Konstanz: Verlag Friedr. Stadler, 1979.

Jackson, G. Gibbard, *The World's Aeroplanes and Airships.* London: Sampson Low, Marston & Co., Ltd.

Jane, Fred T., ed., *Jane's All the World's Airships 1909.* Arco Publishing Company, 1969.

Kirschner, Edwin J., *The Zeppelin in the Atomic Age: The Past, Present, and Future of the Rigid Lighter-than-air Aircraft.* University of Illinois, 1957.

Klein, Pitt, *Achtung! Bomben fallen!* Leipzig: Verlag von K. F. Koehler, 1934.

Knaüsel, Hans Georg, ed:
LZ 1: Das Erste Luftschiff des Grafen Zeppelin: Eine Dokumentation. Freidrichshafen/ Garching: Luftschiffbau Zeppelin, 1975.
Zeppelin und die USA. Freidrichshafen: Luftschiffbau Zeppelin, 1976.

Leasor, James, *The Millionth Chance: The Story of the R. 101.* Reynal and Company, 1957.

Lehmann, Ernst A.:
Zeppelin: The Story of Lighter-than-air Craft. Longmans, Green and Co., 1937.
The Zeppelins: The Development of the Airship, with the Story of the Zeppelin Air Raids in the World War. G. P. Putnam's Sons.

Leichter als Luft Zur Geschichte der Ballonfahrt. Westfälisches Landesmuseum für Kunst und Kulturgeschichte, 1978.

Luschnath, H., *Zeppelin-Weltfahren.* Dresden: Bilderstelle Lohse, 1933.

Mabley, Edward, *The Motor Balloon "America."* The Stephen Greene Press, 1969.

MacDonagh, Michael, *In London During the Great War: The Diary of a Journalist.* London: Eyre and Spotswood, 1935.

McKee, Alexander, *Ice Crash.* St. Martin's Press, 1979.

Maitland, E. M., *The Log of the H.M.A. R 34.* London: Hodder and Stoughton Limited.

Marben, Rolf, *Zeppelin Adventures.* London: John Hamilton, Ltd.

Meager, George, *My Airship Flights: 1915-1930.* London: William Kimber and Co. Ltd., 1970.

Meyer, Peter, *Das Grosse Luftschiffbuch.* Friedrichshafen: Elsbeth Rütten Verlag & Co., 1976.

Mondey, David, ed., *The International Encyclopedia of Aviation.* Crown Publishers, 1977.

Morison, Frank, *War on Great Cities: A Study of the Facts.* London: Faber and Faber Ltd., 1937.

Nayler, J. L., *Aviation: Its Technical Development.* London: Peter Owen/Vision Press, 1965.

Neumann, Georg Paul, *The German Air Force in the Great War.* London: Hodder and Stoughton Limited, 1921.

Nitske, W. Robert, *The Zeppelin Story.* A. S. Barnes and Company, 1977.

Nobile, Umberto, *My Polar Flights: An Account of the Voyages of Airships Italia and Norge.* G. P. Putnam's Sons, 1961.

Owen, David, *Flight: A Poster Book.* Harmony Books, 1978.

Payne, Lee, *Lighter than Air: An Illustrated History of the Airship.* A. S. Barnes and Company, 1977.

Piper, David, *The Companion Guide to London.* London: Collins, 1968.

Poolman, Kenneth, *Zeppelins over England.* London: White Lion Publishers, 1975.

Pratt, H. B., *Commercial Airships.* London: Thomas Nelson and Sons, Ltd., 1920.

Robinson, Douglas H.:
Giants in the Sky: A History of the Rigid Airship. University of Washington Press, 1973.
LZ 129 "Hindenburg." Arco Publishing Co., 1964.
The Zeppelin in Combat: A History of the German Naval Airship Division, 1912-1918. Oxfordshire: G. T. Foulis & Co Ltd., 1971.

Rolt, L. T. C., *The Aeronauts: A History of Ballooning 1783-1903.* Walker and Company, 1966.

Rosendahl, C. E.:
Up Ship! Dodd, Mead and Company, 1931.
What About the Airship? The Challenge to the United States. Charles Scribner's Sons, 1930.

Santos-Dumont, Alberto, *My Airships: The Story of My Life.* Dover Publications, Inc., 1973.

Schiller, Hans von, *Zeppelin: Wegbereiter des Weltluftverkehrs.* Bad Godesberg: Kirschbaum Verlag, 1967.

Shute, Nevil, *Slide Rule: The Autobiography of an Engineer.* Heron Books, 1953.

Sinclair, J. A., *Airships in Peace and War.* London: Rich & Cowan Ltd., 1934.

Slessor, Sir John, *The Central Blue.* Frederick A. Praeger, 1957.

Smith, Richard K., *The Airships Akron & Macon: Flying Aircraft Carriers of the United States Navy.* Naval Institute Press, 1965.

Snowden Gamble, C. F., *The Story of a North Sea Air Station.* London: Neville Spearman, 1967.

Spanner, E. F., *The Tragedy of the R-101,* Vols. 1 and 2. London: E. F. Spanner, 1931.

Taylor, John W. R., and Kenneth Munson, *History of Aviation.* Crown Publishers, 1977.

They Were Dependable: Airship Operation World War II. U.S. Naval Air Station, Lakehurst, New Jersey, 1946.

Toland, John, *The Great Dirigibles: Their Triumphs and Disasters.* Dover Publications, Inc., 1972.

Vaeth, J. Gordon, *Graf Zeppelin: The Adventures of an Aerial Globetrotter.* Harper & Brothers, 1958.

Ventry, Lord, and Eugène M. Koleśnik, *Jane's Pocket Book of Airships.* Macmillan Publishing Co., Inc., 1977.

Von Wiegand, Karl H., and Lady Drummond Hay, *The First Trans-Oceanic Voyage of a Commercial Air-Liner.* King Features Syndicate, Inc., 1928.

Walker, Percy B., *Balloons, Kites, and Airships (Early Aviation at Farnborough: The History of the Royal Aircraft Establishment, Vol. 1).* London: Macdonald & Co. (Publishers) Ltd., 1971.

Wellman, Walter, *The Aerial Age: A Thousand Miles by Airship over the Atlantic Ocean.* A. R. Keller & Company, 1911.

Wykeham, Peter, *Santos-Dumont: A Study in Obsession.* Harcourt, Brace & World, Inc., 1962.

Zeppelin: Ein Bedeutendes Kapitel aus dem Geschichtsbuch der Luftfahrt. Friedrichshafen: Zeppelin-Metallwerken GmbH, 1978.

Periodicals

"Les Dirigeables." *Icare,* Été, 1976.

"Ferdinand von Zeppelin." *Icare,* Été-Automne, 1968.

"Honors to Dr. Hugo Eckener: The First Airship Flight around the World." *The National Geographic Magazine,* June 1930.

Mieth, Otto, "Shot Down by the British: A Zeppelin Officer's Story." *Living Age,* April 1926.

"Santos-Dumont." *Icare,* Printemps-Été, 1973.

Von Wiegand, Karl H., "London Mapped by Yards for Zeppelin Attack that Lasted Only Ten Minutes." *The World,* September 23, 1915.

Picture credits

manities Research Center, University of Texas at Austin. 88-91: Library of Congress. 92, 93: Map by Walter Roberts. 94: From *Histoire de l'Aéronautique,* Éditions de l'*Illustration,* Paris; Stato Maggiore Aeronautica, Rome. 95: Norsk Polarinstitutt, Oslo. 96, 97: Luftschiffbau Zeppelin GmbH, Friedrichshafen. 98, 99: The Press Association, London. 100, 101: Alfred Eisenstaedt. 102, 103: Goodyear Aerospace Corporation. 104, 105: Drawings by John Batchelor. 106, 107: Drawings by John Batchelor and Lloyd K. Townsend. 108: Ullstein Bilderdienst, Berlin (West). 111: Drawing by Theo Matejko, from *Berliner Illustrirte Zeitung,* courtesy Bildarchiv Preussischer Kulturbesitz, Berlin (West). 112, 113: Charles Phillips, courtesy National Air and Space Museum, Smithsonian Institution. 114, 115: Bundesarchiv, Koblenz (2)—Toni Schneiders, courtesy Zeppelinmuseum der Stadt, Friedrichshafen (3); Photo Bulloz, courtesy Dollfus Collection, Paris.

116: Library of Congress, from *Zeppelin-Weltfahrten,* Dresden, 1933; Luftschiffbau Zeppelin GmbH, Friedrichshafen—Deutsches Museum, Munich. 118: From Vice Adm. Charles E. Rosendahl Round-The-World Flight Album, UTD-History of Aviation Collection. 119: Luftschiffbau Zeppelin GmbH, Friedrichshafen. 120, 121: "Graf Zeppelin Over San Francisco" by Stan Galli, © Nut Tree Prints. 122, 123: Luftschiffbau Zeppelin GmbH, Friedrichshafen—Toni Schneiders, courtesy Private Collection, Friedrichshafen. 124, 125: The Bettmann Archive. 126, 127: Library of Congress. 130: The Illustrated London News Picture Library. 131: The Press Association, London. 132-137: Goodyear Aerospace Corporation. 138: Jörg P. Anders, courtesy Kunstbibliothek Preussischer Kulturbesitz, Berlin (West). 141: UPI. 142: U.S. Navy, NAS Moffett Field, California. 143: Goodyear Aerospace Corporation. 144: Erwin Böhm, courtesy Zeppelin Museum, Frankfurt.

146, 147: Luftschiffbau Zeppelin GmbH, Friedrichshafen; insert, Henry Beville, courtesy National Air and Space Museum, Smithsonian Institution. 148: Luftschiffbau Zeppelin GmbH, Friedrichshafen. 151: Luftschiffbau Zeppelin GmbH, Friedrichshafen; Bundesarchiv, Koblenz (3), except top right, UPI. 153: Ullstein Bilderdienst, Berlin (West). 155: Goodyear Aerospace Corporation. 156: Photo Bulloz, courtesy Dollfus Collection, Paris; Ullstein Bilderdienst, Berlin (West)—Drawing by John Batchelor. 157: Armand van Ishoven Archives, Antwerp—Drawing by John Batchelor. 160, 161: Ullstein Bilderdienst, Berlin (West)—Armand van Ishoven Archives, Antwerp. 163: Armand van Ishoven Archives, Antwerp. 164: Bildarchiv Preussischer Kulturbesitz, Berlin (West). 166, 167: Wide World. 168, 169: *New York Daily News.* 170, 171: Wide World. 172, 173: UPI, except center, Frederic Lewis, Inc. 174, 175: Frederic Lewis, Inc.

Index

Printed in U.S.A.